# Only One Thing Can Save Us

ALSO BY THOMAS GEOGHEGAN

*Were You Born on the Wrong Continent?*
*How the European Model Can Help You Get a Life*

*See You in Court: How the Right Made America a Lawsuit Nation*

*The Law in Shambles*

*In America's Court: How a Civil Lawyer Who Likes to Settle*
*Stumbled into a Criminal Trial*

*The Secret Lives of Citizens: Pursuing the Promise of American Life*

*Which Side Are You On?*
*Trying to Be for Labor When It's Flat on Its Back*

# Only One Thing Can Save Us

## WHY AMERICA NEEDS
## A NEW KIND OF LABOR MOVEMENT

Thomas Geoghegan

**THE NEW PRESS**

NEW YORK
LONDON

Requests for permission to reproduce selections from this book should be mailed to:
Permissions Department, The New Press,
120 Wall Street, 31st floor, New York, NY 10005.

Published in the United States by The New Press, New York, 2014
Distributed by Perseus Distribution

LIBRARY OF CONGRESS CATALOGING-IN-PUBLICATION DATA
Geoghegan, Thomas, 1949–
Only one thing can save us :
why America needs a new kind of labor movement / Thomas Geoghegan.
    pages  cm
Includes index.
ISBN 978-1-59558-836-4 (hardback)—ISBN 978-1-59558-865-4 (e-book)
1. Labor unions—United States.   2. Industrial relations—United States.
3. United States—Social conditions—1980–   I. Title.
HD6508.G374   2014
331.880973—dc23                                          2014020463

The New Press publishes books that promote and enrich public discussion and understanding of the issues vital to our democracy and to a more equitable world. These books are made possible by the enthusiasm of our readers; the support of a committed group of donors, large and small; the collaboration of our many partners in the independent media and the not-for-profit sector; booksellers, who often hand-sell New Press books; librarians; and above all by our authors.

www.thenewpress.com

*Composition by dix!*
*This book was set in Fairfield LH*

Printed in the United States of America

2  4  6  8  10  9  7  5  3  1

# Contents

# Acknowledgments

I owe such an enormous debt to the late André Schiffrin, co-founder of The New Press, for inspiring and shaping this book. He died in December 2013. I hope the final product justifies the support he gave me.

And I thank again Sarah Fan, my editor at The New Press. She makes me seem like a much better writer than I am. Once again she has been painstaking and patient—and somehow got this book over the finish line.

My friend Jim McNeil read drafts and gave very helpful feedback. Other friends read parts or all of the book—including Len Rubenstein, Ed James, and Brian Cook. Please don't blame them for any errors or woolly thinking.

Thanks to *The Nation* for letting me write about Keynes.

I am grateful to everyone in our law firm: Mike Persoon, Sean Morales Doyle, Carol Nguyen, Hanna Dworkin, and Emma O'Connor.

Finally, I am dedicating this book to all five of my brothers (and yes, that's right, I don't have any sisters). It's amazing that they turned out to be some of the best people I have ever met.

# PART ONE

# The Case for Rational Thinking

# 1

# "You and I Are Done!"

"So, do you think 'labor' will *ever* come back?"

As a union-side lawyer I hate when people ask that question as if it's my problem and not theirs. You'd think with tears in our eyes we'd embrace each other and say: "My God, what should we do?"

It's a question now not of bringing back "labor" but of bringing back the middle class. And neither you nor I have done enough on that.

In forty years as a labor lawyer, I've yet to figure it out—and now?

"You and I are done," said Ed, who's my age. "It's up to younger people to figure it out."

Well, I'm not *done*. With my 401(k), I have to keep going.

The other day I spoke to the guy at T. Rowe Price: "What do you think? Should I be in bonds? Maybe I should preserve capital?"

He seemed astonished. "You—preserve capital? You still need growth."

I'm sixty-five and I still need growth. That's why at this point in my life the collapse of labor is something personal. When I was younger, I thought of it as a problem for other people. But as I get older, I realize: *I should have either saved more or made sure there was a labor movement to protect me.* As it is, even Barack Obama seems ready to cut my Social Security.

It scares me how many of my friends are scrambling harder than ever. Here's what one told me: "I thought when the kids were gone, my wife and I would have it easy. But somehow both of us seem to be working harder than ever. Those violin lessons I imagined I'd be taking in the morning? Forget it. It's as if someone shows up and shouts in your ear: 'Fine, your kids are gone, they're all through college, great—NOW GET TO WORK!'"

With no labor movement, no pension, what's to become of us? And we're, relatively, well off!

At Starbucks I wince when the little old white-haired lady behind the counter says, "Can I start something for you?"

Start an IRA, for both of us. Only she and I know it's too late.

At least she's working. I have friends my age who have no pension, nothing, and know they will never work again. They hope so, but . . .

"There should be a March on Washington," said my friend Tony, "for all us guys, over sixty, who know we'll never find a real job again."

It's the last act for us: old guys, marching, like the Bonus Army in the Depression. Perhaps, as in the 1930s, General MacArthur will send in horse soldiers to sweep us away—all of us tottering baby boomers who were never in a war.

Of course it's for the young I feel sorry: after all, it was on our watch that a labor movement disappeared. Am I wrong or do they seem intimidated? So far as I can tell, at least on the El, they seem to shrink from one another. They stare pitifully down at their iPhones, which stare up pitilessly at them. Their own gadgetry sits in judgment of them.

But why pick on them? Everyone seems demoralized. In my practice, I long ago came to accept that when labor disappeared,

I'd stop seeing union members. But now they are not even "employees." More and more I have clients who have signed away their rights to be considered "employees" at all—which means there's no minimum wage of $7.25 an hour, no Social Security, nothing. Years ago they should have said something when the HR people said: "You're no longer employees here—but cheer up, you'll go on working for us as independent contractors." In one case we have, the boss even made the guys set up their own personal "corporations," as in "John Smith, Incorporated." Then HR says: "We don't pay you, John Smith, but John Smith, Incorporated." My friends ask: "How can people live on the minimum wage?" But as an independent contractor, John Smith, Incorporated, doesn't even *make* the minimum wage. Sometimes I think: one day, every American worker will be a John Smith, Incorporated, every cleaning lady, every janitor, every one of us—it will be a nation of CEOs in chains. "How did I let this happen?"

At some point, maybe 2034, it won't even occur to us to wonder. We'll just be too beat.

I'm thinking of the road dispatchers we represent—the guys who come out and jump your car if you're in an auto club. They used to be employees; now they're independent contractors, and after they pay for the lease of the truck and the gas, they typically don't clear the minimum wage.

Or we may all end up like the cabdrivers. Right now we have a suit against the city of Chicago, which sets their fares. We're trying to get a ruling that after driving forty or fifty hours per week the cabbies should at least be clearing the minimum wage. They drive, and drive, and drive, up to twelve hours a day, but after paying for the lease and gas many end up under $7 or even $6 an hour, and some go in the hole.

What about tips?

Yes, that's with tips.

It's true the crafty old foxes make more: they know when to

pounce at the Board of Trade. But they have to put in seventy or eighty hours a week. When you're as old as I am, you try putting in those hours.

So in the case of McDonald's or Wendy's, I'm all for raising the minimum wage—to any level Elizabeth Warren wants. But for a lot of our clients, it would be a big deal to make $7.25 an hour, and I don't just mean the wretched of the earth but even "John Smith, Inc."

It's eerie to think that in the famous Great Depression play *Waiting for Lefty* by Clifford Odets, those cabdrivers who went on strike had more rights than many of us do today. At least in those days, unlike now, the cabdrivers still worked for actual employers; at least, unlike now, they could count on getting Social Security.

Aside from often not being "employees" at all, I have seen one other big change in clients over the years: they seem much quieter than they used to be.

By 2034 or 2044, when I'm long gone, they may hardly make a peep. Like the kids on the El, everyone will be looking down or glancing away.

Maybe everyone is exhausted.

The other night I went to a class at Northeastern Illinois University. It's late at night, and the kids come to the night class after a full day at work. I was supposed to talk about being a lawyer, but they were beat, I was beat. Then one young man in the back finally raised a hand: "Where . . . this city, where do you think it's all heading?"

Though I wanted to say something serious, I was too exhausted. I was ready to say, "I don't know."

Come on: give him a real answer.

So I paused. And I gave him a real answer:

"I don't know."

I just know my city, this city, the Chicago of the future, can be scary to contemplate. Like the cities of the Midwest, and most of the South, there's not much mobility here. The private sector is more predatory than ever. The payday loan stores keep spreading, many of them secretly owned by the banks. The Fortune 500 companies have hierarchies more rigid than ever. The kids in this night class at Northeastern Illinois will die when they try to climb those much steeper corporate ladders. In the public sector, there's still a middle class, but it's shrinking because we're selling off the public sector. Chicago's 36,000 parking meters were sold off to Morgan Stanley, and its partners, who keep extending the hours and jacking up the rates. And now that the city has stopped funding the mental health clinics, we have more people hallucinating and wandering the streets. That may be the Chicago of the future, the city into which all of us clutching our 1099s will be descending.

But will it really be so bad? I don't know.

For all I know, an increase in inequality may be fun. It may turn out that the city will be full of laughter and dancing, because we're all poor but happy and no longer care about material things.

Either way it will come down to the same thing: the drop-by-drop disappearance of the middle class.

But might we take some hope from the 2012 presidential election?

Yes, we can: sort of.

To be sure, Obama said nothing about unions or labor. But look at the commercials, the ones that raged at Bain Capital or the notorious video of Romney with his rich friends dumping on the 47 percent. Bain Capital cuts people's wages, and then Romney and his pals snicker at their own workers because they don't earn enough to pay income tax.

Of course Obama's majority is being spun as one based on race or even gender. But at least in those commercials, wasn't the election fought on labor issues?

Bain Capital cut your wages.

Bain Capital is a predator.

That's what went on the air. The Democrats did everything but use the FDR blast against "economic royalists." Even that line might have been in a commercial I missed. Based on the ads, one would think that the agenda for a second term would be labor law reform. Oh, I wish the Democrats had the courage of their commercials!

But here's the sad part: what's been the follow-up to those Bain Capital commercials?

None. There's no plan to let people fight back.

It's true that Obama has nudged up the tax on the top 1 percent, up to a rate of 38 percent, a bump that got the approval even of Grover Norquist. It's also true that Obama has proposed raising the minimum wage to $10.10 an hour—and by executive order put it into effect for government contractors. Still, the mimimum wage is an easy one: it's a way that grateful Democrats can be "pro-labor" without actually having to be for organized labor. But raising the minimum wage absent a labor movement just keeps everything else in place. And so long as everything else is in place, the middle class keeps going down. Maybe Joe Biden would do something more for labor. Maybe—it is half possible to fantasize Hillary Clinton would, in a rash mood. But it's hard to think Obama—*whom I love*—will ever do much more.

Think back to the first Obama-Romney debate, the one that went disastrously for Obama (though he really was not that bad). At one point the moderator asked both men, "What do you see as the role of the federal government?"

Romney's answer was gibberish: Up with People, or something like that.

Obama's answer was that of a technocrat: thanks to the federal government, we have "Race to the Top."

For readers in Seoul or Paris, I should say that "Race to the Top" refers to a program of the U.S. Department of Education to give grant money to states to help improve student test scores. It's the fact that Obama clearly was not "prepped" that made his answer so unnerving. Left alone, on his own, he thinks the most important thing he can do as president is to make us take more tests.

Labor is not Obama's thing—raising test scores is his thing.

But I've no right to talk. In my brief political career I did no better.

Indeed, I write this book as an act of expiation. It was bad enough that a few years ago, idiotically, I ran for Congress; sure enough, I was clobbered. But even worse, during the whole campaign I said almost nothing about the one thing that could save us: the right to join a union, freely and fairly, without being fired. Instead, I ran on other issues: "Raise Social Security." "Put in Single-Payer Health Care." "Stop the Bailout—or Make the Banks Write Down Our Debts."

But I left out the big thing: pass a law to let people join unions, without risk of being fired.

Why not just say it?

I lost my nerve. "People don't want to hear that." "No one runs for office with 'labor' as the issue." Yes, I doubted my own cause. When Moses doubted by striking the rock not once but twice, at least he took some whacks. I was too much of a doubter even to pick up a stick.

I repent.

Of course I know it is the *only* issue. I also know how hard it is to get our left to think so, as we run off to fight for a thousand causes but beg off from the big one. "But it all seems so impossible!" Yes, the Constitution, with its gridlock, is a big problem. But it's not impossible to get a debate going, nor is it impossible to push it as *the* issue of the Democratic Party. Can't we at least get the party leaders to say the middle class itself is being robbed by the nation's employers? But if Obama or Clinton or Harry Reid ever had a concrete proposal for a general pay raise for the middle class, then I missed it. I admit they're getting closer, though. At least there will be a long-overdue tweak of the rules for overtime pay, to cover salaried "managers" and "executives" who may be making just barely over $23,000 a year. But it all adds up to very little. Here's an easy way for the Democrats to raise the spirit of the country—just by *saying*, "Your boss should raise your wage." I mean everyone's wage, not just the busboy who's making $7.25. But they don't. Even Biden, who is by far the best, doesn't go that far. We need not just a sound bite but a whole principled politics over, yes, a right to a higher wage, but also a right to some control over what we do at work. We need a principled politics, with the ardor of the abolitionists, pressed the way they pressed that kind of politics on Lincoln.

Or we can do it for practical reasons. Here are three practical ones:

It is the *only* way to get the middle class out of debt—the private consumer debt that is now structural in nature. It's the debt we have to run up to keep the economy running at all.

It is the *only* way to get the government out of debt—our public debt. To do that, not just the "1 percent" but most of us should pay more in taxes. But it's impossible to extract more out of a broke and bitter middle class. In that respect, the GOP has found the perfect way to shrink the government—namely, to shrink people's wages.

Finally, it is the *only* way to get our country out of its external debt, our trade deficit—we need a new type of corporate model, one based on a labor-management partnership, so we can be competitive enough to reduce the deficit and maybe even run a modest surplus.

Is that enough?

Maybe I should add one more thing: it is the *only* way to hold us together as a country and to stop the growing inequality that in thirty years could bring the whole Republic crashing down.

Go online to Google all the studies and you can get lost for hours looking down, down, into the abyss of our inequality. Even the ways of keeping count of it are becoming uncountable. Let's start with Paul Krugman, whose *New York Times* blog offered this graph showing changes in income shares, 1979 to 2007:

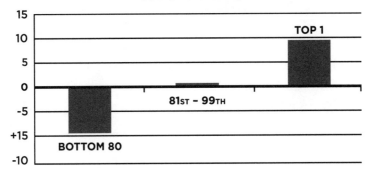

## CHANGES IN INCOME SHARES, 1979 TO 2007

Krugman writes that even most of the *top fifth* are just treading water: "The top quintile excluding the top 1 percent—which is basically the abode of the well-educated who aren't among the very lucky few—has only kept pace with the overall growth in incomes." All the redistribution has been from the bottom four-fifths to the top 1 percent, or really one-tenth of the top 1 percent.

It's not 1 percent: it's *0.1 percent*. Yes, nine-tenths of the top 1 percent struggle like you and me.

Soon it won't even be one-tenth of 1 percent.

I heard a talk by Richard Freeman, the prominent labor

economist at Harvard. He pointed out that in 2011, just *four hundred people* took 16 percent of all capital income gains in the economy. That's not even one-tenth of 1 percent of all the people living in a Chicago ward.

Some say that our current income inequality is no longer like the Roaring Twenties or even the Gilded Age: we're reaching inequality that we haven't known since feudalism. Charlemagne, not J.P. Morgan, is the relevant comparison.

Look at the Gini inequality index, which sets 0 as perfect equality and 1 as perfect inequality. Our index number long ago passed 0.2 and 0.3, which are the numbers of France and Germany. Now it is approaching 0.4, which is the number for Russia and Iran, and could shoot up to 0.53, which is the number for Zimbabwe. The Gini coefficient measures inequality of income; the inequality of wealth is far worse. On November 19, 2012, Daniel Altman wrote in the *New York Times* that as late as 1992 the top tenth controlled twenty times the wealth of the bottom half of the population. By 2010, it was sixty-five times.

If it keeps tripling every eighteen years, then by 2028 it will be 190 times.

That's why in books like *Freefall* and *The Price of Inequality*, the economist Joseph Stiglitz has given a sensible, Ciceronian-type warning that the Republic is at stake. In a *Vanity Fair* piece titled "Of the 1%, by the 1%, for the 1%," he writes of the Arab Spring: "Americans have been watching protests against oppressive regimes that concentrate massive wealth in the hands of the elite. Yet in our democracy, 1 percent of the people take nearly a quarter of the nation's income, an inequality even the wealthy will soon come to regret."

For one thing, he argues that such inequality slows economic growth, so even the 1 percent ought to worry. And here's a scary thought: if growth slows, as Stiglitz predicts, it will be harder for the 1 percent to take all the increase in income. So to keep up their "take," the 1 percent will have to be even tougher about cutting the wages of the middle class.

In other words, then the top 1 percent will have to reach down and grab more from us than before just to keep pace: take not just 95 percent of the income growth, as they did between 2009 and 2012, but more like 125 percent of it in the future.

That's sort of what's happening. As I write, we are literally fifty-eight months into the recovery from a recession that technically ended in 2009. During that time, corporate profits have gone up 50 percent, the Standard & Poor's index has gone up 80 percent. But median household income has dropped by 3 percent.

Dropped, during the recovery.

The economist Herbert Stein is famous for saying, "If something cannot continue indefinitely, it doesn't." But this inequality *could* continue indefinitely. And if we have the income distribution of Russia or Iran, if we are to concentrate the wealth in the way Zimbabwe does, we may end up with political institutions more or less like theirs.

That's why the debate over labor law reform is a debate over the future of the Constitution. "Oh come on—despite the inequality, is there any likelihood we'll 'rewrite' the Constitution?" We *are* rewriting it. In the U.S. Senate, the modern expansion of the filibuster now makes it much harder to pass any law that would change this distribution of income. The curtailment of it in 2013 applies only to presidential nominations—and that happened just so that the government could keep functioning. In the House, gerrymandering has reached a new level of digital perfection, able to shut out Democrats even in moderate states like Ohio and Pennsylvania. Oh, and did I mention *Citizens United*? Now the First Amendment protects money instead of speech.

So *are* you and I "done"? It's easy to think so. Let me set out here one of the arguments of this book. The crisis now is not just the drop of membership: that's an *old* crisis. Rather, even within that dropping membership, the money is running out—and that's the current crisis. Call it the "agency shop," or the "union security clause," or the right to collect dues: it's disappearing. It's true that in the 2014 case of *Harris v. Quinn* the Supreme Court let stand—for now—the use of the "agency shop," which requires even nonmembers to pay a "fair share" of the union's expenses. But *Harris* is also a blistering legal attack on the agency shop. A conservative majority seems as if it's dying to throw it out— someday. And if the agency shop goes away in the public sector, it will—sooner or later, under one rationale or another—in the private sector as well. Indeed, under *Harris* the state could not impose the agency shop on home health aides only because they are too much like *private* sector employees.

Even if the agency shop survives future Court challenges, it may not matter much. More states, like Wisconsin and Michigan, are moving to roll back union security—in just the public sector in Wisconsin and in both the private and public sectors in Michigan. To the extent that such state right-to-work laws increase the number of free riders, labor is more likely to go broke. The whole labor law model is based on the premise that the union will be the "exclusive representative" of everyone. But that takes everyone chipping in. If right-to-work laws keep spreading, labor will not be able to service even the little it has, much less expand.

So we are "done," right? Well, maybe not. After all, for the past thirty to forty years, this model has not really been working. That's how we end up with this plutocracy: the tripling of income by the top 1 percent while wages have stagnated. But maybe we're about to lose the entire thing. Our current American labor law model has been quite good at holding down unions, but conservatives can't seem to leave it alone. If they keep picking it apart, say by getting right-to-work laws everywhere, on top of what they already have, the existing model may collapse. And if that happens, we might have no choice but to put in place something new, such as I hope to describe in the last part of this book.

While coming up with something new could be scary, maybe the young are up to it. Maybe they will stop the magical thinking of the party's leaders, i.e., that we can do something about in-equality without bringing back a labor movement.

As I started writing this chapter, I ran into just such a young person. She seemed out of place at a dinner party for a lot of older lawyer and MBA types like me. I think she was dropping off food for a sibling who was our host. At any rate, she seemed to know I was a labor lawyer and introduced herself.

"And what do you do?" I asked.

"*I'm a labor organizer*," she said.

I dropped my voice: "Really?"

Though I do labor law and I do represent unions, I rarely meet an organizer, least of all at such a dinner party. I had thought half the people in this room were corporate vice presidents. "Where are you working? Who are you organizing?"

She was organizing mostly women, low-wage, Latino. I blush to say that I had to ask the stupidest questions.

"What do you say to them? How do you get them to join?"

Well, though she gave a longer answer, here's the part I remem-ber: "You have to get them to stop thinking, 'Maybe I'll win the lottery.' Or 'Maybe something will come along.' You have to make them see: '*No, that's not going to happen*. But here's this other thing, the union. Maybe right now it can only get you another dollar or two an hour. But even that could make a difference in your life.

"'It could make a difference for *you and your child*.'"

Sure it makes a difference: do the math, like they do at the Ken-nedy School. Another dollar an hour adds up to $160,000 for her and her child over a working lifetime of forty years. We just have to stop the magical thinking: not just of low-wage people at the bottom, or even of those smack in the middle of the middle class, but even or especially of those at the top of the Democratic Party. The case for labor is nothing but the case for rational thinking.

Here's the problem: to encourage rational thinking, what kind of romantic do you have to be? The young organizer at this party—I say "young," she might have been thirty—could have chosen to be an MBA. Instead, she's inside a plant on the South Side trying to get low-wage workers to think like MBAs. I knew the research director at her union. One day I asked about her.

"Do you know her story?" he said.

"No," I said.

"She came to us a few years ago and wanted to be an organizer, and we turned her down. We don't just hire people to be organizers, you know. We said, 'If you want to work for us, go out and get a job in a factory.' Do you know what a 'salt' is?"

Yes, I knew what a "salt" was: you get a job undercover. You don't present yourself as being from the union.

"We do a lot of this," said the research director. "Of course we don't exactly advertise it."

Now that I knew her story, I was aghast. Who would do this? It means that to get people to engage in bourgeois-like rational thinking, we need all these young romantics willing to throw their lives away and live in garrets like in *La Bohème*.

Yet this may be the only thing that can save us. If she and others her age don't throw away their lives and don't make the case for rational thinking, something that cannot go on "indefinitely" may go on *indefinitely*. I'd like to end here with some bit of irony, but at age sixty-five I'm in no mood for irony. It is a dead serious fear that at some point or other in the future history of this country there will be no middle class.

# 2

# "There's No Middle Class!"

I recently met a French businessman, a kind of venture capitalist, living in New York. He found two big differences between the United States and France. "The first—it's so much more open in America. It's so easy to make contacts, to call people up."

"And what's the second about America?"

"There's no middle class!"

Well, it's a joke, but it's less of a joke to say there's no *lower* middle class: the welders, the clerks, who start families on $40,000 a year. They're the ones who took the pay cuts. They're the ones who used to stand between the upper middle class and the poor. Now they are the poor, or the "near poor."

They're even eligible for charity. In my own state of Illinois, we are eligible for charity at a hospital if we are within 200 percent of the official poverty line. Where is that line?

Well, for a family of three, here is the charity line: $39,060.

So let's take a welder, making $17 an hour: with two dependents, that welder and his family are eligible for charity care at a hospital.

But that's not even the worst.

Worse is that some members of the UAW, at least a couple of years ago, weren't even making $17 an hour.

In December 2011 in the *New York Times*, Louis Uchitelle reported that the typical starting wage at General Electric was $12 an hour. At the GE plant in Louisville, that's what people were taking. In Chicago, I met up with Lou and thanked him for the story.

He nodded. "What struck me," he said, "is how passive people are."

It's not just General Electric but General Motors, and even Boeing in Charleston, South Carolina. They were building the Dreamliner at a starting wage of $14 an hour.

But it was especially depressing to me that even the UAW—a union I much admire—couldn't deliver a better starting wage than $14 an hour.

A few weeks later, I saw a client who worked at a Ford plant in Chicago. David is near my age: gray-haired, ponytailed, very muscular, and with a CPA's sense of numbers. He had the gravitas of a banker, and in a former life as a local union financial officer he'd kept a scrupulous set of books.

Why not ask him?

David came for a consultation, and after we had finished with business, and he was about to leave, I said: "Can I change the subject?"

"Go ahead."

"At the Ford plant, here, in Chicago . . . it's really $14 an hour?"

"Yes."

"But there are benefits, right?"

"There are no benefits."

"No," I said. *Don't tell me that.*

"No," he said. "There's no health insurance for nine months. And for thirty-six months, there's no pension, and even then it's just a 401(k)."

"That's it?"

"That's it."

He said that the people making $14 an hour work alongside and do the same work as the people who make $28 an hour.

Wow, that sounded dangerous to me. "And is there any kind of . . ."

". . . 'animosity'? Yes, let's say there is, or could be, a certain— oh, animosity."

He let that word linger.

"Of course," he said, "a lot of these people are glad to get $14 an hour. And now the buyouts are trying to come back to get those very jobs."

Who are the "buyouts"? The buyouts are the guys who took Ford's offer of $100,000 to leave. While he was a union officer, our client was spending his Saturdays and Sundays down at the union hall counseling UAW members over whether or not to take the buyout.

Back then, he had many a conversation that went as follows:

David: "You're sure you want to do this?"

UAW member: "But they're giving me $100,000!"

David: "But after taxes, it's only $62,000. That's *all*. You think you can live on that?"

UAW member: "No, no, don't worry—I'll be starting my own business. That money will see me through."

And now—surprise—some of the buyouts have come crawling back to try to get their old $28-an-hour jobs for $14 an hour. Only now, having signed it all away, they've lost their chance to get rehired.

Yes, I bet there's some . . . animosity—and maybe from the young new hires too. It was a bad time back when David was a local officer, 2008 to 2010. Those were the years when the world was collapsing. That's why he was in the union hall on weekends. "After all," he said, "I'm an S.H. lawyer. At some point I got a degree in it."

"What's an 'S.H. lawyer'?" I asked. I knew it was a stupid question.

"Shithouse lawyer," he said.

At least an S.H. lawyer doesn't run up law school debt.

Now, of course, Ford is back. And while the local was down to eleven hundred people in 2009, now it is up to four thousand.

That's good, isn't it?

"You see, they don't have to move to the South now to get $14 an hour. They can get it right here."

David's right. We're all southerners now.

Does Ford or GM or Boeing or Caterpillar think that you can start a family at $14 an hour? Sure they do. You can start one in a trailer park.

Meanwhile, in Germany, the German workers at BMW, Daimler, and Volkswagen make an average of $66 an hour. That's right: with wages and benefits it's $66 an hour.

In December 2011, in the online journal *Remapping Debate*, Kevin Brown investigated wages at auto plants in Germany and here. He went to our own U.S. Bureau of Labor Statistics, and also talked to the vice president of the big German union IG Metall, which is more or less like our UAW.

In Germany, the total was $66 an hour.

In the United States, it was $33 an hour.

But Brown was using numbers from a year before, when the restructuring of auto in the United States had not kicked in. Since Brown wrote his story, IG Metall has won a 3 to 4 percent raise in pay for autoworkers.

And of course, thanks to restructuring, the U.S. wage is lower. But which country is more competitive: the United States at $33 an hour (and now lower) or Germany at $66 (and even higher)?

Brown pointed out that Germany at the time was turning out

5.1 million cars a year. In the United States, it was 2.9 million. And the German companies export not just within the euro zone or even the EU as a whole but outside it as well. In the United States, we just sell them here.

How can German workers be getting so much more?

Ah!

I'm expected to say: "It's because they're in unions." But it's not so simple. It's also because they're directors of these companies. Because of the works councils and co-determined boards, they have real positions of power.

Or to put it another way: unlike the poor wretches in our country, they aren't "spun off" to run their own little-bitty "companies." They run, or help run, the Big Ones: BMW, Mercedes, and VW. "Oh, that's it. They sit on the board of directors. They're on the works councils. They've got clout."

But it's not so simple.

It's not—as we say in Chicago—that they can clout themselves a higher wage. If they don't deserve it, they can't. Here is the real difference: in Germany, unlike the United States, they can set things up so that they do deserve it. In Germany, unlike here, the people on the shop floor can force or prod or push a BMW, a Mercedes, or a VW to train them, to turn them into superstars, so they can get the wages of superstars.

That's the clout that the German middle class has and ours does not.

When Brown's article came out, *Forbes* interviewed a U.S. economist at the American Enterprise Institute, a right-wing think tank. Why, *Forbes* asked, could the workers get such a higher wage in Germany?

"It's because they can get away with it."

It's just plain old labor power, as raw as it can be. That's what the right thinks; and that's probably what the left thinks. And there's much truth to that. But I'd like to make a different claim: that they deserve a higher wage in Germany because they're higher skilled. And here's the corollary: over here, Ford, GM, Boeing, Caterpillar, and others want us to be lower skilled.

Wait, they *prefer* low-skilled workers?

Yes.

Now that's contrary to what you and I are told; it's contrary to what President Obama, the pundits, and even the companies are saying. It's the world turned upside down. I know it's hard to believe.

After all, if it's true that corporations don't want us to be higher skilled, then it's pretty demoralizing for those of us who would like to push for more education, more job training. What's the point, right?

But before you dismiss the claim, listen to what David has to say about how things have changed over time at Ford. "They have a system there," he said. "I like to call it 'Simplicity.' It's to break everything down into the simplest possible tasks." Indeed, he claims that both the hourly and the salaried positions are being simplified.

By that David means that there used to be skill sets, or different levels of work. In the old labor contracts these skill sets had names, "classifications." It might be General Utility or Repair. The newbies would say, "Hey, I see that guy over there. How can I do what he's doing?" It used to mean more pay. One went to Ford to move up and develop higher skills in order to get more pay.

Well, that's gone.

The "classifications" in general may soon disappear. Or let's put it this way: entry level will be the classification, and people will stay there. Even if people learn higher skills, which used to lead to more money, they will stay at the entry level, at entry-level pay.

And here I'd add that in nonunion places it is even harder to move up. People start at welder at $17 an hour, and they stay at welder at $17 an hour.

There is a puzzle about welder pay, which lately has received comment in the *Chicago Tribune* and the *New York Times*. The puzzle is that there is a shortage of welders, and employers moan about it. But the pay is stuck at $17 an hour, where it's been for years. That means the real inflation-adjusted wage is *dropping*. Even with a shortage of labor, the wage drops.

But worse, after the welder starts and gains experience, the pay does not go up.

As it turns out, somebody's pay goes up. Someone has to be the straw boss. Someone has to watch the other welders. My friend Dick Longworth, now retired from the *Chicago Tribune*, is a much published writer on the Midwest and may be our greatest authority on what goes on out here. He was curious why wages of welders don't rise. He talked to a few nonunion companies. "In the nonunion shops, it's not two-tier, but it's more like a bell-shaped curve." Though almost everyone is clustered around $17 an hour, there's one outlier, the straw boss, who makes a lot more.

These are small shops. There's much more bureaucracy at Ford, where they used to have foremen. Then the foremen became "supervisors." But I'll leave it to David to bring things up to date:

"When I started at Ford, we had these guys called foremen." In David's case, the foreman was black and was supervising both blacks and whites—perhaps a surprising thing in the 1970s, but times were already changing. "At the end of my first week, my foreman came up to me and said, 'Look, white boy, you're going to hurt yourself if you keep doing the job the way you're doing it."

Then he took him aside: he mentored him.

And the old-fashioned foreman actually had the skills to do the job. He had all the skills that the younger employees wanted to learn. He knew all the techniques the younger employees needed to master. He and other foremen had come up through those "old-time" classifications, which are all but gone.

As the years went by, the foremen at the Ford plant gave way to persons who were called "supervisors." Then in turn these supervisors were replaced by persons who were called "managers." These managers were now business types who had none of the foremen's skills or knowledge of the operations. "These were people," David said, "who had never done any of these jobs. They don't have the skills. As managers they have to *guess* at what the skill requirements are."

Since the managers don't have the skills, they manage by making sure things are broken down into the simplest possible tasks. That's how we get to the system that David calls "Simplicity." Since we don't have foremen, we dumb down the workforce to make it simpler for the managers. And there's a payoff for Ford: by keeping down the skill level, or denying any special skill sets are required, Ford can hold down the rate of pay.

So that's why the pay is at $14 an hour and will almost certainly never go up to $28.

If something goes wrong, if there are mistakes, if a less skilled and uninspired and maybe even demoralized workforce flubs something, it's OK. That's why we hire the college grads. We use engineers like my niece. Instead of using their engineering skills, they supervise the high school grads doing nonengineering work.

Everyone in America is "out of classification."

But, in the end, doesn't it work?

Yes and no. Since it's so hard for us in America to get a perspective on it, I'd like to call on another European observer to testify. I can think of no one better than Professor Gerhard Bosch, a labor economist whom I met in Germany over fifteen years ago. He has published a great deal, even in English, about the German and American labor markets. Alas, I have given up going to Europe—it's too hard to get time off—but fortunately for me, I caught up with him when he was doing a stint at Berkeley.

So what does he think?

"It's so bureaucratic, so hierarchical over here," he said to me. "It's almost shocking for a European to go into some of these plants."

I gulped. Yes, it's hard to hear that from a German.

To Professor Bosch, there's another strange thing. "If you talk to American managers, they think everyone on the shop floor is replaceable. The way they organize work here is to make sure this is so. There is no cost in dismissing anyone. If there are really skilled people co-operating together, you would never tolerate this kind of operation."

But, in the end, doesn't it *work*?

Yes, it works because everyone is getting so little pay. But paradoxically it's quite costly to pay so little and have such low-skilled employees. It means, Professor Bosch said, that in America we pay much more for quality control. We pay more for screwups— and it's only a superficial paradox that because our wages and benefits are so low our labor costs are pretty high. And we pay more for all our "managers," who are both over- and underqualified for the work they're doing.

It's true: Ford and others complain about the lack of job training. It's true: our workers aren't very high skilled. But they *can't* be, or at least they aren't allowed to ply those high skills, because then they would be irreplaceable. Ford and others want us to be replaceable.

Sometimes the corporations more or less say so. Recently Caterpillar was in a standoff with the United Steelworkers over pay at a plant that Caterpillar had just bought in Milwaukee. Cat wanted to cut pay from $16 to $13 an hour. Why, said Cat management, should we be paying more to lower-skilled workers?

But that raised a question no one ever asks: why was Cat even hiring lower-skilled workers? It may just want them because they're easier to replace. If Cat workers were irreplaceable, they could make up a real labor movement to fight.

So as David says, the system is Simplicity: everyone stays at entry level, under the watchful eye of the "managers," who themselves have few if any skills and who are now being called "process coaches." Of course there is someone to watch the process coaches, too. And it is all part of a corporate structure, beloved in our country, that puts an emphasis on hierarchy.

Though we can use fancy terms like "flattened hierarchies," we're not getting "flatter" or more egalitarian: we're just flattening more people into entry-level workers. The Ford model or the Caterpillar model or the Boeing model sets the terms and conditions in all our workplaces, more or less. Even though full employment—if we ever get it—could make it harder to fill vacancies, it would still be a hierarchical model. It would still be one in which many Americans are less skilled than their counterparts in other rich countries and are relatively easier to replace. Of course there are exceptions, but we're moving away from the old-style union classifications that rewarded higher skills.

All this just confirms the view of many German observers that Americans don't believe in job training. They aren't being argumentative; they are stating a fact. Of course we *say* we believe in it. We practically scream it to the heavens. Our politicians talk of little else. For years much of the social policy of the Democratic Party has been based on the idea that more education and job training—or "higher skills"—is the answer. Our greatest social scientists, like William Julius Wilson, just *assume* it's the answer for minority-race children trapped in our inner cities. There is no greater disconnect in our national life: we're doubling down on the idea of skilling up people, while many of our corporations are less and less interested in rewarding skills.

As it has dawned on even some Republicans that countries like Germany are different, they have gone over to "see what we can learn." Governor John Kasich from Ohio took such a trip. So did Governor Rick Snyder of Michigan. I bet even Governor Scott

Walker from Wisconsin went over. And they all talk about the same thing: some institute or educational center that the German government had recently set up. Now I take some pleasure in this because when I started years ago to tout the "German model," even some of my friends mocked me: "Germany is toast." "The wages are too high." But a nice big U.S. financial collapse changes everything, and now Republican governors are taking junkets to see what they can learn.

And of course they learn nothing.

My friend J.D. Bindenagel, a longtime American diplomat to Germany, once told me, "People think they can learn from the German model by taking just one thing away from it, but you can't pick at it like that. You've got to take the whole package."

What's different about Germany is not that a few government-backed institutes promote job training but that there's so little of it. Germany has a small higher education sector but a massive amount of job training that *the companies themselves provide*. And the companies keep doing more. In 2008 Gerhard Bosch published a fine article titled "The Revitalization of the Dual System of Vocational Training in Germany," referring to Germany's apprenticeship program, where students are both in school and in jobs, or "training places," within particular companies. That system was supposed to be obsolete: companies just don't make these kinds of investments in the young anymore, experts say. But instead of withering away, it has become even more sophisticated.

Forget the "institutes"—this is all company-based job training, not to make people generalists but to deepen their understanding and engagement with a particular occupation. We think of our job training as something for "slow learners," i.e., basic literacy skills, a kind of glorified high school. In Germany they think of it as "part of the innovation system," i.e., a kind of continuing education or even college in the workplace. That's the strangest part, the hardest for us to grasp. "In the U.S.," Bosch said, "the innovation only comes from the top. In Germany, the idea is that innovation comes up from the bottom."

"What's that mean?" said a onetime CEO friend of mine.

Yes, what does that mean?

It means working people over there really know what they are doing. While they may not have been to college, they are supposed to possess at least some of the skills taught in higher education, such as those of engineers, civil or mechanical. They end up, in a sense, as designers of the production process. They should be skilled enough to invent.

How has the old dual-track apprenticeship changed? According to Bosch, it's been modernized, extending it into one's entire adult life. Often now a company like Siemens will let its employees leave to go to school, or even college, and then bring them back. These companies know that innovation doesn't come just from newly hired college grads. And when they commit to these workers, the workers commit to them in return. In the United States it's practically the opposite. At many companies, we're still wondering whether to do Basic Job Training, because we want to be able to fire people at any time, and in Germany they're at Job Training 2.0, because they have made these long-term commitments. Of course, as I believe Bosch would say—and as any other expert in his field would say—this kind of Job Training 2.0 would be unthinkable without the kind of labor movement that even President Obama doesn't mention.

At any rate, as if to disprove Darwin, we have largely been going in the opposite direction, as David could tell you from his years at Ford. Of course, there is *some* job training; if there were none at all, our corporate model would collapse. And for all my gushing here, the Germans could still do even more, a lot more: for the young, there can never be enough "training places" within a Siemens or another German firm, and many of the young are cut out. But nearly *all* of them are cut out over here. And overall the contrast is still shocking.

Try to imagine, in the United States, any innovation coming up from the bottom. It's hard for us to believe it's even possible. So what is the explanation? Well, I could say, for one thing it's hard to fire people. If people are irreplaceable as a matter of law, they might as well be irreplaceable as a matter of fact; why not make them crucial to the ongoing success of business? I could also say: historically, German companies have a tradition, a sense of obligation, to do this kind of training. Yes, it's easy to say: "Oh, it's a cultural thing." "It's a German thing." Saying so would let us off the hook. But other countries are doing the same. In some northern European countries—like Belgium and the Netherlands—there are works councils, and they all have more egalitarian workplaces than we do, at least in the sense that they still have a kind of unionism, which we can hardly imagine. More and more, the United States will be the exception among the Western nations. The rest of the world is going one way; we're going another. As long as we're the one country where you can fire anyone at any time, for the color of your tie or the color of your tattoo, or for no reason at all, it is hard to see how the really serious job training we cry out for will ever occur.

If workers can't easily be fired, then there is more reason to invest in them over time. They are going to hang around, after all. And the more the investment, the higher the skill level; and the higher the skill level, the more responsibility they should have. That increased responsibility makes them even harder to replace. And *that* in turn not only leads to innovation from below, such as we don't have over here, but makes it more plausible that they should have positions of responsibility on works councils and even on corporate boards. In the large German companies, workers can elect directly *half* of the directors on the corporate boards. It's a system they call "co-determination." And even in smaller companies—where workers elect only a third (!) of the directors—managers still often have to collaborate with works councils, again elected directly by the workers, to decide how things are done.

*Of course* there's going to be more job training in that kind of system—and I mean a kind of training where, if I learn this skill, you pay me more. And that's why the pay can get up to $66 an hour or even higher. When there is more worker control, there is more job training—and vice versa.

But do you think that's what those GOP governors are going to Europe to see?

True, there's always trouble even in paradise: whether in Germany, Sweden, or Belgium, labor and management are always in battles. But as one German on the left told me, "At least we can still look them in the eye."

In the United States, by contrast, we don't even see our CEOs in the flesh, much less get close enough to look them in the eye. Indeed, it's almost comical. There are all sorts of reasons for the relocation of manufacturing to the South, and in other books I have given them. But after I'm done listing all the weighty reasons appropriate for a book on public policy, I'd like to mention this one: our CEOs don't even like to be in the same town with us, never mind the same room. Consider Boeing, with its engineers and machinists sprawling all over Seattle. A few years ago, it began moving the production of the Dreamliner to South Carolina, to get people to build it for $14 an hour. Like any good labor lawyer, I was indignant: why is Boeing moving the Dreamliner to South Carolina, of all places, instead of building it back in Seattle? I raised the question with my friends here in Chicago. "I mean, it's not like these are lawn mowers: it's the Dreamliner. What's Boeing doing down there?"

But maybe I should have also asked my friends, "And by the way, what's Boeing doing *here*?"

Strange to say, the Boeing corporate headquarters is now in Chicago. Just a few years ago, Boeing's top brass moved to the Loop. Not a single plane is made in Chicago; Boeing is still a Seattle-based company. Most of the engineers and machinists are still out there in Seattle.

It's just that the Boeing president and vice presidents decided to leave.

Why do it?

Well, out in Seattle, at Boeing, a common view is "They just don't want to be around us." I was in Seattle a few months ago, and a union staffer with the Machinists said, "They're mad because we go on strike." But it may be more than anger—it may also be contempt. They look down on even the engineers, in some of the ways Mitt Romney and his friends seem to look down on the 47 percent.

Meanwhile, the CEO at BMW in Munich works in the same building where the cars are being made. Yes, he's up there in his office while all that metal is being hammered into BMWs down below. Why would a CEO at BMW want to flee his workers anyway? They elect half of the directors on his board. If that CEO puts in for a bonus that year, some of those workers hammering down below may have to sign off on his paycheck.

Over here, that's not the case. Instead, the CEO is removed from the worker in a way that might catch the eye of some latter-day Tocqueville. That remove may explain why CEOs here are always complaining about the lack of skills but end up nickel-and-diming even the employees who obviously possess them. I admit, my sympathy is with the working people at the very bottom. But let me express a bit of solidarity here with some of the salespeople and middle managers. They also suffer when hedge funds put in CEOs who have no idea what they do. First the golf outing is gone. Then the secretary is gone. Then the guy at the next desk who covered for her is gone. Then finally the end-of-the-year bonus is gone. The job of the CEO is to run the place on fumes, and the more it runs on fumes, the more that all of us gasp for air.

But does our own U.S. organized labor have any relevance to all of this? Sure—as a labor lawyer, I think it does. But we need something radically different than old-fashioned U.S.-style collective bargaining, and we can't hope to raise wages for a workforce that seems perpetually stuck at the entry level without any real control over what they do in their jobs. The collective bargaining of yore now seems so twentieth century—and it was probably already out of date by the time the great UAW president Walter Reuther died in a plane crash in 1970. If he could come back, Reuther would be the first to tell us: we'll never be able to raise wages or bring back real pensions for people who are trapped in these hierarchical types of companies. Although we find it hard to admit, we are more and more replaceable at every level of education, and every skill level.

To recover the purchasing power the country's economy needs, we need a lot more than the old-fashioned wage bargaining that comes around once every three or four years. As the great liberal John Stuart Mill came to realize in the nineteenth century, we need some measure of democracy *within* these companies. And it's not just John Stuart Mill who long ago began to see this might be a good idea: a brilliant thinker like the great political scientist Robert Dahl, a conventional politician like Angela Merkel, and even Pope Francis all seem to get it too. If workers can't get on a corporate board at Boeing or shove aside the process coaches at the Ford plants, we will never organize the workplace so that you and I are irreplaceable, and there will be no saving the middle class—either the bottom half that is already gone or the top half that is disappearing now.

Of course, I'm willing to accept that we need more job training, or at least I agree that we need to make workers harder to replace. Even in America plenty of corporations—albeit often foreign owned, such as Siemens—realize that. We even have some egalitarian companies such as Tom Friedman likes to see. After all, America has a multitrillion-dollar economy, places like Silicon Valley and Austin do exist, and sometimes the U.S. economy works the way all those books they sell at airports says it is supposed to work. One should always remember: like Marx, Tom Friedman is not entirely wrong.

But he is mostly wrong. Too many presidents and pundits keep telling us that we need higher and higher skills to serve a corporate model that keeps pushing us lower and lower and denying dignity to our work.

# 3

# Are We Weak Enough to Fight?

I fear that the U.S. Constitution by itself is enough to keep a labor movement from coming back, with the filibuster, the gerrymandering, and the current Supreme Court now in place. Long ago, at the time of the Missouri Compromise of 1820, John Quincy Adams wrote, "The Constitution is a compact with Hell, and a life devoted to its destruction would be a life well spent." This is a pretty clear-eyed view from one who became president and took an oath to uphold it. Adams was writing in the context of the Slavery Question, which was the Labor Question of his day. William Lloyd Garrison, the avatar of antislavery, had more or less the same view: to resolve the Slavery Question, the Constitution would have to be destroyed. As it turned out, he and Adams were right: the Constitution was a compact with Hell, and it did have to be put on hold, or suspended for four years, while on the fields of battle over 680,000 soldiers died. And it is hard to see how, unless the Constitution is put on hold, the Labor Question in our own time can ever be resolved.

Since the heyday of slavery, the U.S. Constitution has become much better and much worse: much better since we extralegally got rid of slavery and legally gave women the vote and also now have the direct election of senators. In other ways, it's worse. The filibuster is more common than it used to be. While we may elect our senators directly, it is easier to buy them off. Indeed, thanks to *Citizens United*, the First Amendment now guarantees that money trumps democracy. And now that gerrymandering has gone viciously digital, the redistricting of 2010 means that the GOP will control at least the House until 2020. Still, it's the Senate that's worse. Three times in my lifetime as a union-side lawyer—in 1977, 1993, and 2009—labor law reform has passed the House, and three times it has died in the Senate. It's tempting for me to echo the sixth president of the United States and tell younger people that a life devoted to the destruction of the Constitution would be a life well spent.

But I won't say that.

After all, once, despite all the odds, we did get a decent labor law—three of them, in fact, the Norris–La Guardia Act, the Wagner Act, and the Fair Labor Standards Act—but only because the country was in a meltdown surpassed only by the Civil War. Unfortunately, thanks to Keynesian economics, we now know how to prevent total meltdowns, so it's hard to believe we'll ever have such luck again.

Still, even though it's like a really bad relationship and I know I should get out of it, I'm still in love with the Constitution: I have a scriptural-type reverence for the *Federalist Papers*, Lincoln's speeches, and cases like *Brown v. Board*. I can't bring myself to leave the Church.

So against my better judgment, I will write out here as best I can a way to save the middle class and ignore John Quincy Adams on the better way to spend my life. Let's accept the Constitution for what it is and focus on what it does not stop us from doing: creating a crisis for the Democratic Party if it does not commit itself to labor law reform. "What? The Democrats pay no attention to labor. No, that will never work." But I should explain what I mean by "creating a crisis for the Democratic Party."

It means building a new kind of labor movement that will target its strikes and disruption against the Democratic Party.

And here I should confess my deepest sin as a labor lawyer: I actually dislike strikes—against anyone. As a young lawyer for the United Mine Workers, I didn't like them. I dislike disorder. I like to walk inside the crosswalks and I want others to do it too. Nor do I believe that disruption by itself can bring back a labor movement. To go up against *employers* with the idea of "bringing labor back" is futile. Labor is just too weak, far too weak. Be it a Caterpillar or a Ford, the other side can crush us. If that's the point of striking McDonald's or Macy's or Subway or Walmart, i.e., to beat the *employers* directly, I fear the worst.

Yet if the real target is the Democratic Party and not the employers, enough disruption, made up of little hit-and-run strikes, might change the world. Disruption could work if it led the party leaders to think: "The country's out of control!" Democrats in the White House and Congress definitely notice if a strike gets on the news. For one thing, they have to issue a statement, which Republicans do not. I saw it here in Chicago when workers at Republic Windows and Doors had a sit-in at the plant in 2008. The plant had closed with no notice and without the sixty days' pay required by the federal WARN Act when such immediate closures occur. So the workers just refused to leave the plant. Soon the TV cameras were all over it, and President-elect Obama, Senator Dick Durbin, and a raft of congressmen and state legislators were bowing their heads and gravely saying how the workers at Republic Windows had to get their pay. Multiply the disruptions, and we multiply the chances that Democrats make statements, even if these are strikes of desperation, short strikes, or guerrilla strikes with no chance to cripple an employer but also with little risk of loss, since the strikers rush back to work under the protection of clergy before they can be replaced.

Yes, I can hear the grousing: "It won't work." What else is there? Some may say: start a third party. But historically, creating a crisis for the Democratic Party has worked better for the left than starting a new party.

Martin Luther King Jr. did not start a third party. Instead, he and the civil rights movement created a crisis for the Democratic Party—first for the two Kennedy brothers, and then later for Lyndon B. Johnson. They got their way by *not* "winning" in a conventional sense and beating the die-hard South directly but by going out there, getting water cannoned, with Bull Connor turning police dogs on little children in Birmingham in the spring of 1963, and just causing the entire Democratic Party to roil until it had to turn on its southern base and break up the whole New Deal coalition.

Likewise, in fighting the growers in California, Cesar Chavez kept losing—but he was a genius at creating spectacles that forced liberal politicians at the state and federal levels to respond.

It can't work now? It worked in 2013: Fight for 15, the campaign to raise the minimum wage, mounted a series of hopeless strikes that did nothing to move McDonald's. But these losses put the issue at the top of Obama's 2014 State of the Union address. Indeed, Obama's promise to issue an executive order to raise the minimum wage paid by federal contractors seemed to be the heart of the address. It confirms what Frances Fox Piven and others have argued all along, and they're right.

Of course we need Obama and other Democrats to make an even bigger break, as the party did in 1963. Enough strikes—or "bearing witness in the streets"—might also break apart the party, as it did fifty years ago. Of course this time the divide is between conventional liberals and neoliberals. I believe in the end that enough of the party's conventional liberals would opt for labor's side, even though they might hate doing so. For one thing, without some kind of labor movement, the party leaders will never hold together the coalition that kept Obama in the White House in 2012 and maintained control of the Senate, when, with 8 percent unemployment, the party had no right to win.

Is labor strong enough to force that choice?

No, but—again—it's not by being strong but by being weak and losing that labor can tear apart the party. As Sam Adams knew in Boston in the 1760s and Martin Luther King Jr. knew in Birmingham in the 1950s, it might even be better if we lose. The goal is to roil the party, the way the civil rights marchers getting beaten up in the South used to do.

"But you're talking about destroying the Democratic Party."

No: to the contrary, could be the best thing that ever happened to it. As I will try to argue below, the party needs a labor movement not just to win elections but to govern the country, or at least keep it from cracking up. Even a split could help the party. Even if people like Robert Rubin defect, they might create a more rational center-right Republican Party. A diaspora of erstwhile Democrats could be a good thing for all of us. It is in the interest of the left not to have a right that is just the Tea Party, and Democrats too have a stake in having, if not Rockefeller Republicans, then more Republicans like either James or Howard Baker. Even if we actually tried to split the party, I doubt many Democrats would leave. To be sure, neoliberal Democrats seem to be rife in D.C., but they also like their jobs as aides, lobbyists, and speechwriters. If they think it's in their interest, they may well sign on to the next orthodoxy that comes along.

Besides, the party may be ready for a civil war. After all, for all its weakness, labor still has its friends—maybe as few as Tom Harkin, Sherrod Brown, and Elizabeth Warren in the Senate, but many more in the House.

But who in labor can lead the kind of disruption that would get the party's attention?

It's certainly not the AFL-CIO, although I have the highest regard for many who work there. Some of the member unions have already given up. Harold Meyerson, one of our best political columnists, has pointed out that many unions in the AFL-CIO have decided just to stop organizing.

Twenty years ago the old Big Labor was just wasting away. Now it seems the patient has stopped eating altogether.

But it might be just as well, since that Old Labor is not capable of creating the kind of new labor movement we need: what we need is not just to raise wages but to give people more rights to determine the way we work. So who can lead that charge?

Well, of course, there are some *good* unions: I especially like UNITE HERE, the hotel and restaurant workers. *They* get the idea: do quickie hit-and-run strikes and get out and back in safe, before hotels like the Hyatt can slam in permanent replacements. Under the Wagner Act, workers really do have some rights. By law, hotels like the Hyatt must take back one-day "lawful" strikers if they seek reinstatement before Hyatt can scramble to replace them. So UNITE HERE and the Service Employees International Union (SEIU) have "little" strikes that last no more than a day.

And I especially admire the SEIU for striking so many fast-food places at once, all across the country. Is there a media market they missed? The organizers here—who do seem to be young people—understand the importance of spectacle, even if it is being downsized into Twitter.

But still, this isn't the disruption I have in mind—no, because, however laudable, it isn't the kind of disruption that will split the party, even if the Hyatts of the world are owned by Democrats like Penny Pritzker. It's still the Old Labor just trying to raise the minimum wage. It doesn't really threaten anyone. To be sure, I'm for raising the minimum wage, and $15 an hour sounds threatening enough to me (even if it comes across as the opening gambit for, maybe, just $12 or $11.50 an hour). Yes, we should get out and march, because at $15 an hour, we might start to feel we have a chance to be like Sweden.

And yet even if it got us halfway to Scandinavia, it would *still* be the Old Labor. It wouldn't challenge the basic corporate model. It wouldn't be anything new. Indeed, even with our corporate model, it's a bit surprising that service workers in particular aren't making more. I have a friend who works in management for the City of Chicago, and at lunch the other day he put the puzzle this way: "The building trades do a good job for their people—they get them $45 an hour. Why can't the service worker unions do better than $9 or $10 an hour? Of course the people in the building trades have more skills, but the service workers are doing *something*—there shouldn't be *that* big a gap!"

As wonderful as it may be to raise the pitiful wage at McDonald's or Wendy's—and it's something we should fight for—it's still just a raise in the minimum wage: it's not *that* threatening. It would hardly roil the Democratic Party. I am arguing for disruption that might actually split the party, or at least alienate the party's neoliberals, because disruption would challenge our whole U.S. corporate model. In particular, we need more explicitly political strikes, such as the teacher strike in Chicago I will describe later in the book. So long as they're big, and visible, it does not necessarily matter if we lose or fail to "win" that much by them. It seems to me the goal is to build up to a 1968-style political fight to force the Democratic Party to sign on to a revamping of corporate law—for example, one that might call for electing workers to corporate boards or provide some check on the workplace before robots replace us all. We're not there yet; labor is not there yet. But it's the only way, in a gilded age, with a dysfunctional

Constitution, to stop the top tenth of the top 1 percent from taking more and more.

It's not enough to get up to $12 or even $15 an hour: instead, we have to front the idea of power sharing. And when I try to think of a single group of workers who seem most capable of raising that issue and going out in the street over it, who would be a kind of vanguard for a *new* type of labor movement and even, yes, "storm the commanding heights" (if I could use that old Marxist phrase), who could set the agenda for labor now the way the UAW back in Reuther's time used to do. I find it hard to think of any group better than—

The nurses.

Yes, the nurses: after all, in the age of Obamacare, Health Care is now our "King Coal." Just as Coal later gave way to Steel and Auto, the leading sector now is Health. Look at the fastest-growing occupations according to the U.S. Bureau of Labor Statistics, and roughly half of them are in health care. Think of audiologists, medical secretaries, mental health counselors, and home health aides; there are many others.

If labor is to come back anywhere, it should start here. Right now I would bet on nurses to be the vanguard.

More than most working people, the nurses have the nerve to start a fight. Indeed, they start fights with each other. Look at National Nurses United (NNU), which used to be the California Nurses Association (CNA). They're now in a civil war with the American Nurses Association (ANA). The old CNA decided the ANA was not militant enough and split off from it, and then the ANA, fighting back, became more militant too. Some in labor scorn the NNU, think it underhanded or destructive, but whatever people on the inside may think, from the outside it looks like *all* the nurses are spoiling for a fight. I am astonished that nurses who seem so nice at work—I just had a surgery—seem so angry out in the streets. I mean the NNU marched at the NATO summit held in Chicago in 2012.

NATO?

Well, labor radicals show up at such things, and some of them happen to be nurses.

They aren't out for a bigger paycheck. They want a bigger say in how they do their work—in how they care for patients, in nurse-to-patient ratios, in how long patients are allowed to stay hospitalized.

So I wanted to meet someone actually organizing nurses. Besides, I was curious for a personal reason: the nurses—all of them, in the NNU and all the other nurses' unions—were the only unions that had endorsed me in my run for Congress. Why? I don't know. Maybe it's because they are as frustrated as I am and just didn't care I was such a long shot. A friend of mine went to an NNU convention. "It's astonishing," she said, "to look out and see these nice middle-aged women out there calling for the most radical political change."

That's what I wanted to ask John, the organizer to whom the NNU referred me: "They seem so militant—why are they so different?"

"I know," he said. "I've been an organizer all my life. I've worked with cannery workers. I've worked with lots of low-wage immigrants. But the nurses—it's so different from any organizing I've ever done."

"Yes," I said. "What's so different?"

"OK, first, the majority are women," he said. "So there's not that macho thing to deal with."

Boy, I bet that's a relief. It's strange about the macho thing: in this country it leads to a kind of self-emasculation: oh, I don't need a union.

"And there are other objective differences. Nurses are quite well educated. It's not easy to get an RN degree. But the big thing about nursing is . . . it's a *compassionate* profession. People who become nurses, they want to give something. So the conditions of the workplace are different."

"What do you mean?"

"I mean nurses depend on each other."

They have come to depend on each other even more, he said, now that the "bean counters" are in charge of running the hospitals.

Cut the nursing staff. Make everyone run faster. The patients are sicker. There are fewer nurses on the floor.

But that's not the worst of it, John said. "Remember, they aren't dealing with widgets. In pediatrics, they see the babies, quite sick babies, being pushed out the door because their mothers have a cheaper kind of health insurance.

"So add it all up. You have people with a high degree of education who depend on each other in the workplace. And they are dealing with human lives. Sure, they have their own issues, like cost-of-living increases and pensions. But they make a good living. That's not why they organize."

They see what's going on.

"The hospitals cheat. They cut corners. And it's the nurse who looks in a dying woman's face when the hospital is trying to push her out the door. And she thinks, 'Hey, this isn't what I bargained for.'"

He paused.

"And that's when they call us."

Ah! Here's a nice kind of labor movement: one to storm the commanding heights and show compassion to a dying woman. What better way to throw away one's life than by doing that?

But then John said something that disheartened me a little: "There's one *other* thing about nurses, about why they organize. In some of the big-city hospitals, the majority are immigrants. They're from the Philippines or Nigeria. Compared to native-born

Americans, they have a higher degree of political sophistication. In Nigeria, they know what a strike is. And in the Philippines, they've been under martial law. So they're not freaked out by political confrontation."

Perhaps the foreign-born are simply less likely to accept the U.S. corporate model: the cost cutting, the hollowing out, the subservience to the bean counters. They draw the line at nursing mothers being tossed out on the streets. But most nurses unite on one thing: in return for learning those higher skills that we demand in this global economy, they want to use those skills the right way—or they may withhold them from us all.

That's not the "old" collective bargaining; it's new. It's about the governing of these hospitals. The nurses might just have the clout to elect some of their number to corporate boards. At any rate, they're capable of the kind of disruption that most unnerves the public. And that's the kind that will most unnerve the Democrats and make mandarins in Washington think that the country is out of control.

But is that the only example—the nurses?

Oh no—I saw an even better example at disruption with my very own eyes.

# 4

# "How About Them Apples?"

Indeed, as I sit here at my desk, I'm still getting over the shock. At last, in my old age, I saw a true strike, big and breathless, right in front of my eyes, right in my hometown. For ten days in September 2012, the Chicago Teachers Union (CTU) was on strike, and it was covered around the world. Shortly after it ended, I had lunch with a friend, a scholarly professor, who gave an impartial thoughtful analysis.

"Well," I said, "what did you think of the strike?"

"I *loved* the strike!" he said.

See? That's thoughtful. And that's what I thought: I *loved* the strike! Before, I'd been wondering if I'd ever see one again.

Of course, a strike is a risky thing, and God knows, in my youth as a lawyer for the United Mine Workers, I saw many of them go awry, but . . . it's still hard to imagine a labor movement without them.

*Nunc dimittis*, as Simeon says in the Gospel—although, unlike him, I'd like to stick around.

Believe me, I had nothing to do with this strike and had no

role in the bargaining. I didn't even get one of those 26,000 red T-shirts: one for every striker. I was just a bystander.

But for the previous two years, somewhat to my surprise, I had been one of the lawyers for the CTU. Our little firm filed the CTU's suit in federal court to stop teachers from being not just "laid off" but in effect fired, where they had no right of recall of any kind. Do you think it's hard to get rid of a tenured teacher? In fact it's easy. The board of education has been laying off thousands of teachers—some of the very best in the system—and bringing in raw rookies off the street to fill positions that the laid-off teachers could fill.

Two years ago, to stop these effective firings, we went to court for the CTU. We even won an injunction in the U.S. district court, and then we won again in the U.S. court of appeals. But in the end we lost.

Most of these teachers, by the way, had "excellent" and "superior" evaluations. Some were really the elite of the elite—teachers who mentored other teachers. Why would they get rid of the best teachers and bring in new hires off the street?

Money, of course, but it was also to break the CTU, or to make clear to every teacher that she could be tossed out at any time.

Oh, I wish we'd won that case!

And, now disgusted, the teachers—the clients I had failed—were on strike. Of course, the right to recall was only one of many issues. The strike really arose from a feeling that the mayor and his liberal billionaire friends wanted to fire teachers en masse and privatize the public schools.

In that sense, it was a political strike, like the strikes that fill up the streets in Paris. And that's why people like me said, "I love the strike." We loved the strike because it was giving the finger to Rahm Emanuel, Obama, the whole managerial culture they represent: Bill Gates, Jamie Dimon, Penny Pritzker, Bain Capital, Teach for America, and that whole bunch.

Stephen Lerner of the SEIU argues that the only strikes that work now, like the 2012 Houston janitors' strike, are political strikes, which are not just for the strikers but for the entire community. Well, the CTU strike was a brilliant political strike, and it worked because it was not simply a strike for more money, tenure, or a better evaluation system. It worked because a lot of people—above all, parents who had kids in the public schools—saw it as a strike in favor of good old-fashioned neighborhood public schools.

A few days after the strike, I dropped in for dinner at Tre Kronor, a little offbeat Swedish restaurant, and tacked up on the billboard under the map of Sweden there was a message from the CTU to all the diners: "Thank you for supporting the strike."

It was assumed the diners supported the strike, and they probably did. That was the moment I really knew the CTU had won.

The Sunday night before the strike I had worried, since I'm a lawyer, and they are my clients, and I'm supposed to worry. Ah . . . *a strike?* But Monday morning I woke up and walked past Blaine Elementary School and then Lake View High School, and it was a glorious late-September morning. I took my morning walk, and I saw all these teachers outside in red T-shirts, which made me admire whoever the quartermaster general of the CTU may be: they all looked so good! And they had their Starbucks cups, since this was the North Side, and it seemed impossible that these teachers of first graders and kindergartners at Blaine would be so pumped up, pumping their signs:

"CTU"

"We want smaller class sizes!" (I still see that sign planted in a neighbor's front yard.)

"Honk if you want more arts education."

And people did honk. They drove past the Music Box, with all the Iranian films showing, and they honked. They honked from tractor-trailers. They honked from BMWs. They honked from all sorts of cars. Thank God, I thought: they're honking.

Our side is going to win!

But this was only the first day, and later that day I spoke to a teacher, a very thoughtful, Seven Sisters type of woman who seemed anything but political. *She* was worried.

"I worry how the media will portray us."

I could tell she was already flagging.

It's hard to be on strike after 8:30 or 9:00 a.m. That jolt of Starbucks wears off. It's exhausting to stand around and do nothing all day. On Election Day I used to work the polls, and it's much the same thing. Precisely because there is noting to do, and because the sugar highs keep wearing off, many a striker is a wreck at the end of the day; it's hard to imagine getting up the next day and having nothing to do again. For the sake of solidarity, I was tempted to get in my car and drive from one school to the next and wave to the strikers. It seemed treason to sit in the office. Besides, I was curious to get a gander: it's shameful to say, but for all the time I spent on our CTU case, I had very little idea how teachers *looked*. Some on the picket line looked like those joggers in spandex who cut in front of me at Whole Foods, some looked like Trotskyite intellectuals, and a few just looked like your good old uncle Charlie (albeit your uncle Charlie who watches Rachel Maddow every night), but all of them were on strike or had voted for a strike—not just 60 percent, or 70 percent, or even 85 percent, but way over 90 percent (and remember, there are 26,000 teachers). That's what made this a different kind of strike: it was a strike by my neighbors, the kind who end up running the condo board. Who could be against them?

Of course, there were endless press stories about the unfairness to parents who had no place to send the kids, but polls showed that the large majority of the parents supported the strike. True, most white parents were against the strike, but most white parents send their kids to private schools. Black and Latino parents whose kids go to public school, some of whom actually need the free breakfast programs, were largely in favor of the strike. Why not? They know that some of the first-grade teachers have up to forty kids in a class. They don't have the wherewithal to send their kids to faraway charters and leave work early to pick them up after school. Still, the news media struggled mightily to rattle them—"No one cares about your children"—but most parents seemed to grasp the teachers were striking because in fact they *did* care.

*Children* supported the strike.

Children held up picket signs saying, "I Don't Like You, Rahm."

But it was a young teacher who held up the meanest one: "Rahm Likes Nickelback." A spokesman for the mayor had to issue a statement that he did not.

Talk about a strike against the Democrats—isn't this the kind of strike I'd wanted? I should have gotten in my car and gone from school to school and honked. But of course at 9 a.m. or so on that Monday, I went off as usual to the office, which is downtown, in the Loop, across from city hall, and sat there like a slug. "I should be out there." Then at about 3 p.m., I could hear the noise, and someone in our office said, "They're all out there marching," and I went downstairs and out of the building and saw thousands and thousands of teachers marching past the Picasso, where the kids skateboard, and pouring down Clark Street, ten or fifteen red T-shirts across, and heading for the board of education. I started walking with them. I looked over and saw Tom Balanoff, who is the international vice president of the SEIU and whose dad I used to represent, and I would have expected him to be with a phalanx of people, but he was there, alone, happy just to be a marcher like everyone else.

I waved. "Hey, Tom, how are you?"

Tom said, "Look at the cops. They're all in favor of the strike." Yes, the cops want a contract, so they don't like Rahm either, and I thought: "He's lost control of the 'narrative.'" Wait—what am I saying? He's lost control of the *city*. It was not just the mayor or the aldermen but the CEOs and the *Chicago Tribune*—they all had lost control of the city. I felt sorry for a moment: up there on the fifth floor of city hall, Rahm Emanuel must feel like the czar in the Winter Palace. I had to keep walking to stay ahead of the teachers so that they, like a red cavalry, would not ride over me, and I passed my barber, who had climbed up on a big stone wall to watch. "It's interesting," he said, "to put faces on all of this."

They were *your* teachers, for God's sake. You could stand at Clark and Madison and look north and south and think: here comes everybody. That's what a strike does: it brings into history for just a second all sorts of people you never get to see. I represented the teachers, and even I didn't know that there were so many of them. There they were, in red T-shirts: "CTU Strike, 2012: How About Them Apples?" The elite tell the media and the media then tell us what we're to believe, but the spectacle of these highly educated people in the streets put in doubt everything they've *ever* had to say. Why didn't the elite or the media prepare us for this? "Oh, the good teachers won't strike." But they *had* to be striking, because at Clark and Madison it seemed everyone was striking, all of them wearing red T-shirts, one big massive line of red that seemed to go on for miles.

As I stopped and stood there, and gave up counting, I thought of what my friend Hector had once said about Occupy Wall Street: "Yeah, well, it won't make any difference, until the people making $80,000 a year come out to march. I mean these guys who finally say, 'I've had it. I don't get any vacation. I don't have a life.'" Since these teachers make almost that much, I wish Hector could have been here so I could say: "*Now* what do you think?"

And there was another way that this strike was more threatening than Occupy Wall Street. Unlike the children of OWS, the teachers did have a specific, political demand: "Don't privatize the schools!" Oh, there had been teacher strikes before, but never one like this. In that way, it was even better than a strike of guys making $80,000, because those guys would just be striking for themselves: "I'm mad as hell and I'm not going to take it." The teachers were stand-ins for all the people who were too poor to go on strike. Think of the issues the CTU tried to bargain over:

There are not enough textbooks.

There are up to forty kids in a class.

The paint is peeling, and whole wings of the buildings are closed.

The mayor keeps cutting back on mental health counselors and social workers, whom so many kids desperately need.

In that way, the teachers are like the nurses: their strikes come not just out of anger but out of compassion. Perhaps at this moment, only caregivers like teachers and nurses have the nerve to stand up to the plutocracy.

After the CTU pulled off the strike, some of the billionaires threw a fit. One of them, Bruce Rauner, an Emanuel adviser, gave a speech at the George W. Bush Institute the day the strike ended. Obviously irked by the mayor's sensible decision to give in to the CTU and try to take back control of his city, he was quoted in the *Chicago Tribune* on the need to rally everyone to go out and break the union. "I think we're going to have a multiyear *revolution*. . . ." He was *sure* that the teachers could still be split over merit pay. Surely the good teachers would one day come over to his side. "The good teachers know they'd do fine. They've got confidence. I've talked to them. . . . You've got to break apart the union bosses from the really talented ones."

At any rate, in the case of president Karen Lewis and the other CTU officers, the "union bosses" *were* the "good teachers." Two or three years ago, they had just been teachers in classrooms. Running as outsiders in the last election, they'd come up from the rank and file.

I can understand why the billionaire types were so aghast. To them, it was a shock the CTU was in the streets. Earlier in 2012, they had been crowing: "We just passed a law that will make it impossible for them to strike!" For months, a YouTube clip showed one of their lobbyists, Josh Edelman, boasting that he had more or less "bought" the Illinois General Assembly (a plausible enough claim) and pushed through a Wisconsin-type law that made it much harder to get a strike vote: no longer by a majority of the members, as before, but by an absolute 75 percent of *all* teachers in the schools, whether card-carrying members of the CTU or not, whether or not they had cast a vote. If only because of so-called good teachers on the side of the billionaires, or teachers who just wouldn't vote, it seemed impossible that the CTU could strike.

"Ho, ho, we fixed their wagon."

I have never seen such a miscalculation of the enemy.

More than 90 percent of all teachers, in and out of the union, voted to call a strike. In a certain way, by passing that law, the mayor and the billionaire "reformers" helped the CTU conduct an even better strike. Raising the bar, they made sure the CTU leaders would spend even more time going to every member, bringing in every teacher they could.

But didn't they also put limits on bargaining?

Anything to "organize the workplace," as nurses seek to do, violates the law. Does the CTU want a smaller class size? That's an "illegal subject of bargaining." The board wants at least thirty students in a class and even defends having forty—and these are the poorest kids, many of them traumatized by street violence, some with autism, severe emotional disabilities. Never mind: forty is fine. Any bargaining to help the kids? It's illegal.

Remember, there are 386 school districts in Illinois, and Chicago has the second-lowest tax rate—number 385. That means just about everything is off the table.

Under Illinois law, teacher pay was about the only subject over which the CTU was allowed to bargain. The CTU's line was "Oh, we're still bargaining over wages." But they weren't. Indeed, just before the strike ended, the board went to court to argue that the strike was really over "illegal" demands.

The mayor himself mocked some of the CTU demands—"They even want to strike over the lack of air-conditioning in the classrooms"—and pointed out that the temperature that particular day in September was only in the seventies.

It was a bon mot worthy of Marie Antoinette. By the way, in July and August, when the track E kids, who go to school year-round, are in class, it's often over ninety degrees, and the board now is putting air-conditioning into the schools.

So what made it a political strike also made it an illegal strike. OK. Go ahead. Sue. Get a court order. What was he going to do—turn on the hoses?

Yes, I'm a lawyer, and I'm responsible enough to know how a no-strike injunction can destroy a union. So spare me the e-mails. I know too well what happened to the Mine Workers, where the wildcat strikes went much too far.

But from the mayor's point of view, he was hardly in a position to start making mass arrests. Besides, he's not just a Democrat but a "national" Democrat! Had he turned on the hoses, he would have destroyed himself politically. With Obama running against Romney, the last thing he needed was a brawl in the streets of Chicago. So yes, the mayor did end up engaging in "illegal" bargaining.

So here's the first lesson of the CTU strike: the best kind of strike is one that targets the "national" Democratic Party, or at least gets its attention.

A second lesson may be: every strike now has to be "political," in some way. The labor movement has to open up its strikes, like parades, so others who watch from the office windows can come down and run along.

Some may object: "Most strikes don't lend themselves to being political." The challenge is to get across that *every* strike, whether it's by nurses, teachers, janitors, Walmart cashiers, is a "political" strike. It's a matter of volume: if there are enough strikes, then every strike is part of the story. And again, because labor is so weak, these have to be guerrilla, hit-and-run strikes, out for a day or two, and everyone run back. Right now, these kinds of strikes occur and get a smidgen of attention, but they will never work until there are enough of them to get every one of them in the news, because then, at last, there will be a 24/7 story that "the country is out of control," even though it's not.

A third lesson may be: just one good strike keeps on giving. Just after the strike, Eric Zorn, a brilliant columnist for the *Chicago Tribune*, tried to add up who "won" and who "lost" in the CTU strike. He decided it was the CTU in a "squeaker." But I demur: it was the CTU in a roar. By just looking at "issues," like the teacher evaluation system, we miss something bigger— the fact that the strike has created something new in the city, a movement, or even a kind of opposition party to the mayor. It put into the streets for the first time, in those red T-shirts, teachers and young people and a lot of lost millennials who never dreamed they would be in the streets. It let little children, it let barbers and bankers, it let the whole city see the mayor and the billionaires lose control of the city. For many, an image of red T-shirts is now silk-screened in their minds. To crib here from Don Rose, the city's great activist and campaign manager who has led marches since the 1950s, that will pay off in elections and marches for years to come.

So why didn't it work that way with Scott Walker in Wisconsin? Perhaps it did.

At first blush, the attempt of the left to throw out Governor Scott Walker looks like an argument against disruption. After all, when Walker tried to limit the bargaining rights of Wisconsin public employees, there were marches, rallies. Wasn't this a political strike that flopped?

Political it was, but it wasn't a strike. Unlike the teachers in Chicago, no one ever walked out and no one ever engaged in a strike, except perhaps the Democratic state legislators, who tried to deny a legislative quorum and went down to Illinois to hide.

Maybe I'm unfair. To strike against Scott Walker would have been illegal, because the public employees were under contracts with no-strike clauses, and they could have been discharged. But the CTU strike was illegal too, and by striking the CTU took a big chance. In Wisconsin, they didn't. To be sure, they had good reasons not to take the chance: after all, the CTU had spent years pumping up the rank and file for the expiration of the contract, while in Wisconsin, Walker's attack caught labor unawares. Anyway, I wasn't there, and I have no right to second-guess. Here I am, not far away in Chicago, and during the entire uproar I didn't go up to march, unlike Bea Lumpkin, my client Frank Lumpkin's widow, who went up every weekend, and she's older than I am. So I have no right to talk, and yes, if the idea was to throw out Scott Walker in a recall election, then maybe even a short strike would have alienated too many voters.

In Wisconsin that was the strategy: not to strike but to fight for labor in an election. And as it turned out, although Walker won and it wasn't even a "squeaker," it was amazing that labor even got that close. After all, the recall was really an up-or-down vote on labor as *an institution*. That is, it was not over the right of, say, teachers or nurses to use their skills, but at least in part over the right of labor as an institution to force everyone to pay dues, whether they like it or not. The "old" labor model depends on this kind of compulsory tax, either the full membership dues or the "fair share" equivalent that every employee has to pay, whether in the union or not.

In America, it is hard to think of a worse issue on which to raise a popular insurrection! But in Wisconsin, that in effect is what labor wanted to put up to a vote. Really, what were they thinking? It happened, just as disastrously, in Michigan as well. The rich can buy elections. The Koch brothers *do* buy elections. If I were a second in a duel, advising on the choice of weapons, be it election or strike, and saw a labor movement about to choose the former, I'd be shouting to the skies: "Don't pick that one!"

Remember: no country has ever gone to the polls to *vote in* a labor movement. Even in the 1930s, it was the work of a small minority.

So at least one lesson from Wisconsin is: let's not do recalls. And maybe a second is: if we do a recall anyway, never, *never,* make the issue whether labor can take out your dues money without your consent.

Still, maybe we have made too much of Wisconsin. Maybe in the end, despite all the bruising, labor will get a boost in Wisconsin. One union staffer in Illinois told me, "Before the Walker thing, the unions up there were on autopilot. After Walker, some of the officers had to get off their duffs and for the first time in years go out to see their members."

There is also the counterexample of Ohio: by referendum, voters rejected a new state law that would have limited public sector bargaining. Ah, so labor *can* win an election! But no one with money had anything at stake in that particular election. Should Ohio limit public sector labor? Private business in Ohio didn't care. The Koch brothers stayed out. No incumbent GOP governor was going to be ousted. All that Ohio proves is that labor can win an election if there is no one on the other side—or at least if labor outspends the other side by three to one, as it did in Ohio. But how many elections can labor win if the other side outspends labor by three to one?

And that will happen more and more.

If Wisconsin was no disaster, Michigan was. In Michigan, under a relatively nice Republican governor (no Scott Walker), the state went entirely "right to work," in both the public *and* the private sector. That is, the state legislature has prohibited even the "agency shop," i.e., the system by which unions get full membership dues or a "fair share" equivalent (usually 80 percent or more of the full dues) from every employee they represent. Now every single contribution in Michigan will be voluntary, just like at church on Sunday, if you happen to go to church. In Michigan, unlike Ohio, private business *does* have a stake—get rid of the agency shop, and the unions in the private sector become much weaker, just like in the South.

Yes, just like Alabama or Mississippi, *Michigan* is now a "right-to-work" state, and we're talking about the state that bankrolls the UAW. That's David's UAW, the same UAW whose members— until the nurses came along—used to "storm the commanding heights." Not only are the UAW newbies down to $14 an hour, but the dues money needed to get workers back up to $18 an hour is gone or partly gone. The UAW is like an army that has lost its granary. The baggage train is gone. Unlike Wisconsin, Michigan really *is* a big deal, because the old labor model depends on the agency shop, this kind of compulsory tax, whether the full dues or a fair share equivalent. It is this special right of "taxation," if I may use that term, that pays for all the number-crunching staffers, baby-faced organizers, and elderly lawyers hanging on like me—really to pay for everything that makes organized labor such a responsible bargaining partner capable of stopping random acts of rage. Once gone, as in Michigan, that system of collecting money is not coming back. At least any comeback will be much harder than in Ohio, because now business has a stake in the outcome, and the chamber of commerce will fight furiously to stop the return of the agency shop in the private sector. The Koch brothers will weigh in now—not that the chamber of commerce really needs them—and once the commercials roll out 24/7 (and not just on Fox), it's hard to see voters turning out to save compulsory dues.

But get rid of that old system, the union shop, and there's no money, and no staffers, and no embittered lawyers like me; and that means there will be no way of organizing or representing the middle class in any form, so there will be nothing left but people heading for the hills.

To be sure, that may also bring disruption, but not the kind I have in mind: with labor completely gone, little guerrilla actions may pop out of nowhere, with acts of sabotage that have nothing to do with unions or even in pursuit of a rational goal. All that will be left is rage.

"Oh, but that can't happen here." Oh, yes, it can happen here, if there is no organized labor of any kind where people can go.

It's true, perhaps, that I make too much of Michigan. Yes, of course I doubt that the "end of labor" and "guerrillas in the hills" are about to happen now or are even near at hand. But if labor's money runs out and if we see the last of a "responsible," truly *organized* labor, this kind of sabotage or worse may start to happen in the lifetime of many readers. It's true—and it's quite annoying to some of us who like to write these polemics—that it's just impossible at any point to see beyond two or three years ahead.

But there is plenty of reason to worry if Michigan and the like bankrupt what's left of labor. It is a very bad time to lose a labor movement as the U.S. economy enters a new era of permanent "low growth," as economists like Robert Gordon of Northwestern now claim. In this new era, Gordon writes, the GDP growth will be less than half of what the growth rate was for 1950–2007 and even some earlier eras. Tyler Cowen and other economists seem to agree. Suppose this Malthusian prospect is happening. For the middle class, what does that mean? It means that for the top 1 percent to keep up their predatory lifestyle, they have not only to take *all of* that GDP growth (as they do now), but to start doing some serious raiding of the piggy banks of middle-class millennials.

Then there will be disruption, but it may not mean our millennials will be out in the streets or have any specific political goals at all. We may end up either pillaging and preying on each other—or perhaps even worse, turning on ourselves.

This is part of the disruption to come, maybe the most insidious part, is the kind that comes from not doing anything at all. The case for disruption now, the case for more CTU-type strikes, is to fend off the disruption likely to come—not just mindless sabotage or theft of property, although there could be a lot of that, but also the kind of disruption carried out in Melville's story "Bartleby the Scrivener," by an even more passive workforce that will say like Bartleby, "I would prefer not to."

If we really are paralyzed by our Constitution and there is no majoritarian way to break the gridlock, there is only one way out: political disruption, though I hope kinder and gentler forms than one sees in other, less-well-off countries. What else is there? It is an honorable way out. It even has some conservative credentials. Or at least the conservative Francis Fukuyama argues it is a respectable option in his very well written and bestselling opus *The Origins of Political Order* (2011). While he makes the point in general historical terms and not in terms specific to the United States now, he happens to make it just after he discusses the current gridlock in the United States.

If there is to be real political disruption, better that it come now, before organized labor disappears. And it is quite possible it will disappear. If nothing else, it may just run out of money. Without the power to "tax," it may lose the power to survive. Think of the Roman Empire: it declined not so much because the barbarians invaded but because it lost the ability to collect taxes in the provinces and therefore to pay for and field an army. Well, perhaps after Michigan no more states will "go south," i.e., become right-to-work. We'll never lose Vermont—or at least I hope. But we may lose the agency shop in the public sector of all fifty of the states.

After the Supreme Court decision in *Harris v. Quinn* in June 2014, the agency shop in the public sector seems to be hanging by a thread. But the thread may hang for quite a while. In the months leading up to *Harris*, there was panic that the Court would find agency shop in the public sector unconstitutional. Sure enough, in *Harris* the majority opinion by Justice Samuel Alito started out that way: it went on and on—and *on*—attacking the 1977 Supreme Court decision in *Abood v. Detroit Board of Education*, which had upheld the agency shop. Then what? There was *Abood*, all teed up, fat and juicy, ready for overruling, and then . . . nothing. After huffing and puffing to blow the house down, the Court left *Abood* alone. It left the agency shop as before. The dissent even ribs the *Harris* majority for not following through and overruling *Abood*. Except for home health aides—excepted because they are somehow not "true" public employees—just about everyone else will go on paying dues just as before. I feel terrible for the poor home health aides who lost their right to unionize like everyone else. But otherwise, it would seem the agency shop is safe, at least for now.

Better Court watchers than I think the knockout is still to come, however. And they might be right. Should one or two more conservative justices join the Court, the agency shop really will be gone.

Meanwhile, the status quo for labor is not much consolation.

And the agency shop may well go on dying by a thousand little nicks, slowly, state by state.

But labor *can* survive. Members can still contribute voluntarily; not even the First Amendment can block that. And many will contribute, just the way churchgoers put money in the plate at church. For one thing, from auto clubs and groups like AARP, the AFL-CIO has learned to "sell" memberships, with motel discounts and the like. Here's one reason to join: if you get a union card and you have a mortgage at Chase Bank, you can skip five monthly payments on the mortgage in a row when you go out on strike. Seriously, why don't we strike more if our friends at Chase are ready to stand behind us? Think of all the people whose homes are "under water." They should pay dues, yes? And some people do. But on the other hand, just like at a church, many put nothing in the plate—and I include those who really like their unions.

That's what bugs my friend who is a staffer for a teachers union that is in an Illinois "downstate" school district that does not allow agency shop. She asks the nonpayers: "Don't you like what I do?"

"Yes, of course, but why should I join?"

"Well, you'd be a member, and you'd get to make decisions. Don't you want to make decisions?"

"Oh, you're all doing such a great job—I don't see why you need *me!*"

Still, labor will survive to some degree, since some will go on paying dues. But it's going to be much harder to come back. It would all be different, though, if Congress would change the law to let unions represent more workers. Or put another way: if the "base" were bigger, then labor could make just as much money or even more from voluntary dues. Telemarketers and candidates for office can tell you that much—from personal experience I can tell you—it's a numbers game. The more people you can hit up, or guilt-trip, the more money you raise. That is, if only 30 percent of 3 million workers in a group of bargaining units are paying dues, labor is in trouble. But if 30 percent of 33 million workers are paying dues, labor will have not only the same money but a bigger reach than before.

If the Court knocks out dues, that's one way labor can survive: by passing a law that will make it easier for labor to organize.

"How likely is that?"

It's not likely unless there is a wave, or even an era, of political-type strikes.

But there's a second way to survive: start a parallel labor movement, one that exists *inside* the companies. I am referring to European-type works councils and co-determined boards. I don't mean to say that this labor movement "inside" the company can replace the labor movement "outside" the company: it can't. But the labor movement "inside" the company can prop up the labor movement "outside" the company. How? Well, except for wages, it can handle just about every workplace issue—firings, start times, etc.—since that is what works councils do. If nothing else, corporate democracy saves labor's cash, which can now go toward lobbying in Washington rather than paying lawyers like me to defend workers in contract arbitrations. Let the works councils decide.

And here's another big plus about corporate democracy: it's free. No union has to pay for it. On works councils and co-determined boards, the company is paying for all that time. It solves the money problem.

"But how likely is that?"

OK, not likely but possible, if the Democratic Party makes labor *the* issue. Even in America, a party of the left could be "for" labor. At least we can dream! Long ago, it was assumed that there could be "no socialism in America"—meaning, in effect, workers here would never organize. But the New Deal came along, and—

They did. But that happened in part because New Dealers pushed workers as much as workers pushed them—and the New

Dealers, the young, on-the-left ones, who might come from the Kennedy School today, did so in the belief that without a labor movement the country was ungovernable. How do we get Democrats in Washington, at least the younger public policy types, to think the same today?

Perhaps I am refusing to face facts. Perhaps the CTU strike I offer here as a model is just a freak occurrence, at least in the particular way it set up a confrontation "between Democrats." But if it is hard to find strikes quite as rattling as this one, it is possible to imagine there being far more strikes, not big ones, but short ones, one day, two days, even out for a week, at places where no union contracts are in effect. In the summer of 2013, there was a little boomlet of picketers in the Loop: not just at Wendy's and Subway but outside the Palmer House in downtown Chicago, when union busters came to speak. But there still aren't enough little strikes: there have to be far more if we're going to split the party.

The bad news is: rarely can union members do the striking. Whenever they're under a contract, our members can't strike! Yes, I am enough of a labor lawyer to realize that in those circumstances a strike is illegal.

But the good news is: there are fewer union members left. Most people are unorganized, so there is a glut of companies that can be targets of hit-and-run strikes. And maybe one can imagine—if not next year, then in two or three years—that the entire left of the Democratic Party starts supporting these strikes as labor itself runs out of money.

It's not necessarily organized labor that ought to own these strikes. The CTU strike was more of a "political" strike, because it pulled in parents and others in the community. But if these are not always "labor" strikes in a strict sense, labor has to be in the middle of them or they will never get the attention of Democrats in Washington.

"It's impossible, not enough people in this country are ready to go out in the streets."

Most people *don't* have to go out in the streets.

The great steelworker leader Ed Sadlowski once told me how his dad used to go around to guys in the steel mills before a strike and say, "Look, I'm not going to ask you to picket. I'm not going to ask you to march. All I'm asking is that you do nothing. Next Monday, when it comes around, *just stay home.*"

Really, what's so disruptive about that?

Some friends of mine say: "Yes, but if that's the answer, what's the point of lawyers like you?" I suppose my answer is that lawyers can disrupt too. In America we use lawyers to think our way through things. There has to be pressure, just as the abolitionists pressured Lincoln. But in the end, Lincoln and others had to think their way through it legally. That's true in the case of the civil rights movement, too, but that pressure was more effective because Supreme Court decisions like *Brown v. Board* gave it more legitimacy.

And that's how labor came back in the New Deal. Lawyers such as Clarence Darrow and Felix Frankfurter and many others made a devastating legal case explaining why the use of injunctions to stop strikes was wrong. Far from being an essential part of the rule of law, so-called government by injunction was actually at odds with it.

Courts are the place we go to tell the stories that start to change the way we think.

Yes, I worry about touting disruption, especially against Democrats. Sure, I worry that going out in a premeditated way to split the party may backfire. It may go way too far, or not far enough, or do both, in disastrous sequence. But I also worry that with the money running out, labor has so little time. Before we disappear, we in labor have to appeal to the conscience of the party.

Yet we also have to appeal to its brain. We have to lay out an argument that the case for labor is not just a sentimental bread-and-roses thing or even simple justice to the party's base. It is also an instrument of public policy. It is a way of managing an economy. It is a way of preserving a standard of living. That's the case we have to make: no government in its right mind would do away with organized labor as a way of stabilizing the country.

Indeed, even some on the Democratic left need convincing. They see the priority as taxing the rich: that is, income redistribution. For them a labor movement is part of that. But it's not. It comes ahead of it. If the history of the New Deal teaches anything, it's that there is no way to redistribute income until we first redistribute power.

That's why it's the first duty of every Democrat to bring a labor movement back.

# 5

# The First Duty of a Democrat

I took a trip after being clobbered in my run for Congress. Someone from the Clinton County, Iowa, Democrats had called to ask if I would speak at their annual dinner.

"Why would you call me? I just made a fool of myself by running in this election."

"We know," he said. "We figured you wouldn't charge us anything."

So I took I-80 to drive out to Clinton. I thought it could be my last chance to give "The Talk" I kept giving to people rushing past me to the El.

I went past Dixon, Illinois, Reagan's hometown. I could have moved to Dixon about the time Reagan got in the White House. That's what a Loop lawyer once said to me at lunch: "You'd have been one of the only lawyers out there. You'd do all kinds of cases you never do in Chicago." Yes, but what would I do at night? "Oh," he said, "you'd have to get married first to someone up here or you'd go crazy." Or else you'd turn to drink, like Grant did in Galena. But I didn't go—I should have gone. Then I snapped out of it, because all of a sudden I was crossing the Mississippi.

The Mississippi!

Father of the Waters, the Mother of the Interstates. There it was, down below. It's sad: it was the Mississippi that got this country rolling.

Now all that brown sludge is barely moving.

It's global warming, some people say.

Dice are the only things rolling on this river, past towns that lost all their industry long ago.

I drove over the islands in midstream. They are bird sanctuaries, I hear—in fact, that's where the great American bald eagles now are. My brother told me.

"Really? They're down there?"

"Yeah," he said. "They're on those islands somewhere."

They're in an Elba-like kind of exile. I wish I could see one fly.

Maybe they're too downhearted—things seem sluggish in the heartland. Or at least I felt a little down as I drove into Clinton.

It's the sight of an Arby's in place of a factory that always has that effect on me.

That's what is depressing: there are no assets on the ground. Recently a friend who is in banking was telling me, "Even in the 1980s, all the lending in this country used to be 'ABL.' Do you know what that is?"

"No."

"ABL: it means asset-based lending. But it's become a huge problem now, because there aren't any assets now the way there used to be—there's no equipment. There's not enough 'there' there to do ABL."

"So how do you do it?"

"Well, we pretend to do it."

I think he means new kinds of financial instruments.

When you get to Clinton, you see why we have to fake the ABL. Here, in Clinton, Iowa, is where all that equipment used to be. It was Clinton that had the auto plants. It was Clinton where we made not just cars but farm implements and machine tools, and it was Clinton that shipped those materials around the world. When our country was not a debtor but a creditor nation, we Americans had Clinton to thank. Now all that's left of that time is a giant Archer Daniels Midland plant, making corn fructose syrup.

Yes, that's what we're making now in the heart of the heartland: that crap we put in Cokes. All of that glop you get at the Taco Bells.

It's Clinton, Iowa, that's supersizing our kids, in the new workshops of America:

Steak 'n Shake
KFC
Baskin-Robbins
McDonald's

Over the Taco Bells, a single ADM plant looms up like some ancient pyramid. It's Aztec-like, in a way: a corn-based civilization. We just pour fructose syrup into our kids instead of offering them up as human sacrifice.

I had to keep driving out to Weldon, where the Clinton County Democrats were actually holding the dinner. My host told me, "For years we had them in Clinton itself, but people outside of Clinton started saying, 'Oh, it's always in Clinton—that's so elitist.'"

Yeah, well, that's the hit on us Democrats.

Weldon is tiny—it's just a gas station and a joint called Buzzy's Tavern with a sign saying, "This Buzz is for you." When I walked in, I got a Bud.

In the dark I looked for Democrats. For a while there were just a few girls in cutoffs playing pool. But then they came—elderly,

white, Medicare Democrats, Kennedy-Johnson Democrats, beef-
and-mashed-potato Democrats, Iowa Democrats with American
flag lapels. I spoke with a woman who looked like Eudora Welty.
The people here still knew where to find the post office.

The Buds and the beef went around. When I got up to speak,
it was hard not to burp. It's so great to be an American, but when
I got up and thought of the Mississippi not rolling, I knew what
I had to say:

"Ladies and gentlemen, the first duty of a Democrat is to defend our country.

"And that's what we as Democrats have to do, after all these
years of Republicans trying to wreck it. Look at the trade deficit
we run—every year, it's nearly a trillion dollars. Look at the down-
sizing, the closings of all the plants.

"We have to get this country out of debt—not just personal
debt, or federal debt, but the debt we pile up each year to every
other country in the world.

"Here we are in Clinton tonight—"

(*Oops: we're in Weldon.*)

"—and what do we really make? It was Clinton, Iowa, that used
to make the things that helped us pay our way in the world. . . ."

Here came the line where I could see people looking up.

"We're in the clutches of our foreign creditors. . . . We have to
get the independence of our country back."

Some might interrupt my speech here and say I'm overstating
things. It is true that manufacturing has come back a bit—but
only a bit. We're still down from where we were in 2007, a time
when it already seemed we were at an industrial rock bottom. But
don't interrupt me. Tonight I was on a roll.

I was back to being a labor lawyer: once again I was pushing
labor as the only thing that could save us.

First, it's crucial for the long-term economic survival of the country. We need labor-management partnerships, such as Germany or even Japan has. There's historical evidence that countries succeed or fail based on the "inclusiveness" of their economic institutions. A recent well-received book, *Why Nations Fail: The Origins of Power, Prosperity, and Poverty* (2012) by Daron Acemoglu and James Robinson, makes the same claim. If we fail, it's because we've cut people out of decisions. The more people who make decisions, the better countries do.

Look at the recovery from the financial crisis of 2008: the countries that are "inclusive" did better than countries that are not. It undercuts the argument in *This Time Is Different* (2011) by Carmen Reinhart and Kenneth Rogoff. No matter what countries do, they write, it takes seven to ten years to dig out of a financial collapse. We're still digging out. But in Germany, or Austria, or Sweden, which have labor-management partnerships, it took all of about two years.

Second, more people making decisions is crucial to our long-term psychological survival. We can't go on treating half the country with contempt.

Third, it's crucial to the long-term survival of the Democrats. I mean, *who are we for?* Yes, we won the last election, but a national party needs a plan to keep the nation from cracking up. The other day Tom Friedman spoke at a school where a professor friend gave this report: "He said, 'There is no room in the economy for average people.' Well, Democrats better make room because average people vote."

(Really, I like most of Tom Friedman's columns; it's just his riffs on competitiveness that get to me.)

That's my pitch to the Democrats, the "real" Democrats, the people here at Buzzy's Tavern. But here's a question: even if the "real" Democrats out here did want a labor party, would they have the clout to get that across in Washington?

They may be the people who knock on the doors in the

primaries. But they aren't the White House aides, the Office of Management and Budget types, and the Kennedy School grads who decide day to day what "the Democrats" really do.

Do these people at Buzzy's Tavern have any pull with them? No.

Just a few weeks ago, in Washington, I had dinner with a good friend who helped to bring me to my senses. Every time I come here, some old D.C. acquaintance stops me when I gurgle on about this or that grand vision for the Democrats and says, "Do you *know* what is going on in this town?"

This time, a friend who knows the town was scathing about the chance that the Democrats here—the ones in the White House or in the Eisenhower Executive Office Building who make all the under-the-radar rules—would ever take up labor as a cause.

Let me lay out his points:

First, labor law reform will never pass. Forget it. Thanks to gerrymandering, the House will be Republican for at least eight years, to 2020, and maybe a decade beyond.

"No one's going to waste time on that," he said. "So what can you do by rule making?"

"Well, not so much," I said.

"Then I don't see any hope."

Second, these higher-up Democrats just don't care about labor's issues. Does the president ever speak about the right to organize?

Finally, he said, they don't see the 2012 coalition as having anything to do with labor, the way I do. He thinks they just got lucky because Romney happened to be a terrible candidate.

I said, "But he was so terrible because he was a plutocrat."

He dismissed that claim—and he might have a point.

I had to catch my breath. It was a shock to come to D.C. and realize how few Democrats in high places are really friends of labor. My friend—who really does know D.C.—was quite right to point it out.

In part, that's the fault of organized labor. Union leaders seem clueless about getting prolabor Democrats into power. Perhaps on hearing this, the members of the AFL-CIO Executive Council would splutter. It could be true that a labor leader can still get a meeting at the White House.

I bet Joe Biden takes those calls. But is there any effect on policy?

Look at the U.S. Senate: there are currently fifty-five Democrats. But apart from Tom Harkin and Sherrod Brown, there may be only two or three more who even grasp what a union is. To be sure, there are many more union supporters in the House of Representatives. And even senators can appreciate organized labor as a kind of PAC fund, a source of money. Perhaps even more than the rank and file, they dislike a right-to-work law: it disrupts the flow of money to their campaigns. It's arguable that Democrats in Washington would rather roll back the right-to-work laws than roll out a right to organize.

But with the money labor spends, why does it have so little clout?

You have to say this much for the old Communist Party of the 1930s or the Mafia: at least they knew how to get their people into positions of power. By comparison, organized labor is a flop. Perhaps I dare not cite my own hopeless campaign for Congress. Perhaps I deserved not to be endorsed by any of the unions except the nurses. Some didn't know me. Some said I didn't have a chance. And some were miffed that I had sued unions for not being democratic enough.

But if not me, they could have found some other labor person to run: it was a special election and, as it turned out, the winning candidate received only about eleven thousand votes. Labor could easily have delivered enough votes for a union officer, union staffer, or union lawyer. Then at least there would be one such person in Congress!

Finally, it hit me: they just didn't care.

"Oh, we're for Representative X, because he did us a favor on a bill in Springfield."

Or "We're going with State Senator Y, because she helped us on a nursing home issue once."

So they split among two or three candidates. One union officer told me, "It's not like any of them are going to be against us."

Right, so it doesn't matter. Congress is probably full of Democrats who aren't going to vote *against* labor unions. But how about a Democratic Party where at least a third to a half of its legislators live and breathe for just one thing: to bring back a labor movement?

But that didn't even occur to anyone. Then when I go to D.C., I hear people in labor say, "Oh, they don't pay attention to us at the White House."

Really, how can you blame them? It's astonishing how inept labor is at putting in its own people.

This is a disaster because, like it or not, the labor movement *to some extent*—I hate to say this—has been a project of the elite. In our history, sad to say, it's at least arguable that Big Government was responsible for what used to be Big Labor. I know many on the left refused to believe it: no, no, the people rose up, etc. Indeed, my friend at dinner assumed I thought so too: "I suppose that the 'proletariat' will rise up?"

I could have said, "Well . . . there are precedents."

But I partly agree with him: I do think we need those White House aides to help bring back a labor movement. And while disruptions and strikes are important, they're important because that's how we get the elite in the Democratic Party to take on labor as a project.

Before my friends on the left blow up at me, let me explain why I think the revival of labor is at least *partly* a project of the government. Here's a graph that shows the rise and decline in union membership. Let me ask readers to look at two segments of this graph, 1936–40 and 1941–45. Just see where all the growth occurred.

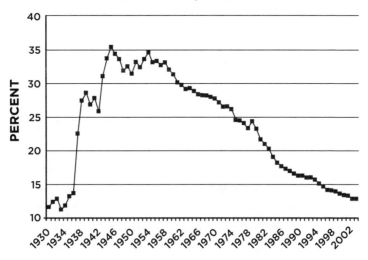

## UNION MEMBERSHIP: PERCENT OF NONAGRICULTURAL WORKFORCE, 1930 TO 2002

The first spurt, 1936–40, came after Washington, D.C., had cleared the way. It started four years *after* the enactment of the Norris–La Guardia Act, which took away the power of the courts to issue injunctions and left employers exposed to wildcat strikes, sit-ins, and other strikes that would be illegal now. But there was no labor movement that knocked down the door to get this kind of radical change; it came from middle-class progressives, the great-grandparents of those who graduate from the Kennedy School today.

The first spurt also came *after* FDR had already tried a kind of European co-determination, or had at least given labor a role in setting industry-by-industry "codes." I refer here to the National

Industrial Recovery Act of 1933, or the Blue Eagle Act. Yet when Roosevelt pushed this enormous expansion of labor's power, there was only a tiny labor movement in place.

So it's worth noting: only two to three years *after* the New Deal pushed this huge expansion of labor power did workers "rise up" and have sit-ins at Flint, which Democrats like Governor Frank Murphy effectively encouraged by leaving the sit-in strikers alone.

But that's a small thing compared to the role of New Dealers in creating the second big spurt in labor membership, in 1941–45. That second spurt rivals the first. But there were no sit-ins. It was World War II. To strike was illegal, as well as unpatriotic. Nor was the National War Labor Board giving out wage increases. There was a clampdown on prices *and* wages. So if the romantic view of things is right, how could this possibly be a time of labor's biggest growth? One could say, "It was the wartime spirit," and to be sure there's much truth in that. But to break that down, in practical terms, it was a command economy, and businesspeople knew that the New Dealers wanted them to have unions. Look at the Office of Price Administration (OPA), where the young John Kenneth Galbraith would decide which CEO could or could not raise prices. In 1942, a businessman who wanted a price increase from the Democrats in Washington would have to be a damn fool not to have in place a union. What young New Deal price controller would otherwise give him a break? Even in the 1950s, many businesspeople were still boasting of their good relations with unions.

It was not just acts of disruption or people pouring into the streets, though I am sure those actions pushed the New Dealers to go further. The point is: they *did* go further. Yes, they were young, on the left, and they probably went to plays by Clifford Odets. But they also wanted a labor movement for a hardheaded reason: to bring order to the country. They wanted to stabilize the economy, to stop the gyrations and swings that had ended in the

Great Depression. They saw, correctly enough, that they needed a labor movement to govern the country. To use the jargon of our own day, they wanted "inclusive" economic institutions, as any government should, so that more people are involved in making decisions.

While some on the left may not like to admit it, the increase in union membership was partly a project of the government—of the thirty-something White House types who come out of public policy schools today.

It's true even now, as I mentioned above, that we still depend on government to push people into unions. Whenever labor has a success—and it may be a small thing, like dibs on a construction project at Dulles Airport outside of D.C.—it's often because an elected Democratic officeholder made it happen. That's why it's a disaster if White House types, the public policy grads, or even readers of the *New Yorker* stop thinking of labor as the answer, the only way to hold down inequality and bring stability to the country. It's a disaster when Obama or Bill Clinton thinks the answer to what we used to call "the Labor Question" is just to have more competitive tests.

On the other hand, I know it's disheartening to think that we need the government to push people into unions. It is a fair question for public policy types to ask: "Wait—why can't they just do it on their own?" In Europe, or at least in western Europe, labor movements seem to pop up pretty naturally. So why does it have to be a special government project over here? Some say, "It must be American 'exceptionalism'"—a term, by the way, that apparently not the Tea Party but Joseph Stalin was the first to use. But, like the term "globalization," "exceptionalism" sounds like it explains something when it doesn't. Of course there are always other "factors," as we learned when we wanted to ace our exams: if we want a decent grade, better to list ten or more. But since this book is pass/fail, let's just discuss the Big One: fear—the fear that comes from the threat of violence, physical violence or even the verbal violence that spews every day out of Limbaugh-type talk radio, which aims to bully not so much women or even minorities as hapless white males who hang around these guys. In the history of our country, there's just been too much violence to have a "normal" labor movement. Sure, now we're down to genteel mass firings, and for exam purposes I could go on to list ten other factors we have to consider as well, including "learned helplessness" being passed down meme-like from Generation X to Generation Y. Still, the Big One looming above them all is fear: that's why most people dare not even put on a union button, much less pick up an actual picket sign. So if it takes a village to raise a child in Africa, it takes a government to bring back a labor movement over here.

Of course one may ask: why should Kennedy School types care?

The answer is: they get to keep their fabulous jobs.

The Democrats who hire them get to stay in power.

That's what I tried to say to my friend in D.C.: "Well, it's in their interest to do what the young Galbraith and others used to do. Democrats like Obama and others—they have to offer something. They can't just go on pitching this idea that all of us should go to college. At some point, people out there in the country won't buy it."

"They seem to have bought it so far."

"Well, at some point, they're going to stop—and I'm . . . I'm talking about the Democratic officials and party people at the tertiary level—"

"The 'tertiary level'?"

"I mean people who knock on doors and things—"

Yes, the people who showed up at Buzzy's Tavern. They need a better message to carry door to door.

But do I really suppose that active Democrats at this "tertiary" level are going to change the way the rising-star White House or OMB staffers or Washington types think?

Even as I tried to argue why it might happen, I lost heart. Of course, I'm being ridiculous. I doubt the people out here in Weldon—the ones who do the phone banking—ever really get heard. OK, it is ridiculous. But let me dream. And I'd like to suggest that maybe, just as a matter of logic, the White House and OMB types and all the rest might come to this way of thinking on their own. In part it's why I bother even to write this book, in the hope that maybe a public policy student would take a break from doing regression analysis and download it on a Kindle. Maybe it could be boiled down to something tweetable, like:

All your number crunching isn't working, and it won't without a labor movement.

As a postlabor party, the Democrats are supposed to be the party of the welfare state or entitlements. They exist only to protect Social Security and Medicare. But without a labor movement, it's in doubt whether the Democrats in the long run can even hold on to those. It's difficult to keep a welfare state or maintain entitlements without a middle class to tax. As that middle class disappears, we'll have more fiscal cliffs and battles over debt ceilings in years to come. It's doubtful the party can save entitlements, at least at the levels we once expected or that exist in many other high-income countries.

If they can't save the welfare state—and they already seem to be working on ways to cut back on Social Security—it's hard to see how the Democrats have a future as a postlabor party.

Even more seriously, Democrats have no way to get the country out of debt: personal debt, public debt, and the trade debt that goes on bleeding us hollow every year. Without a labor movement it's impossible for them to deliver for the middle class.

But then I come back to what my friend in D.C. asked: even if that's true, and even if one could convince the party's elite, what could they really do?

Look at that spurt in union membership after 1941: when a Rotary Club businessman had to beg a young whelp in D.C. to get his prices up at all. Yes, World War II is over, but on a smaller scale there might be a chance to push labor again. Despite what I told my friend, rule making or an Executive Order can still help. There is the President's authority over federal contracts. Under the Procurement Act, the president has broad discretion "to provide for the Government an economical and efficient system for . . . procurement and supply" (40 U.S.C. §471). The federal government does a lot of spending—in the 2013 fiscal year, $460 billion in federal contracts.

How to use this clout? Frustrated that labor law reform died in Congress, Bill Clinton did try to use this clout to help labor. On March 8, 1995, he issued an executive order that would have barred employers that busted their unions—or, to be exact, would have barred employers that permanently replace lawful strikers." But in *Chamber of Commerce et al. v. Robert Reich*, 74 F.3d 1322 (D.C. Cir. 1996), the U.S. Court of Appeals for the District of Columbia, a very conservative federal court, put an end to all of that. And it was easy to do. After all, the president was effectively punishing employers for engaging in something that was perfectly legal under the National Labor Relations Act—that is, a right, with some exceptions, to hire replacements for strikers. That made it easy to say that the president was interfering with the exercise of a legal right "protected" by federal law, or at least by a long line of court and National Labor Relations Board decisions.

It was also punitive and crude and had the look of a big payback to the AFL-CIO. The public never heard of it. No one made a big deal of it. I wonder if Clinton even remembers doing it at all.

On July 31, 2014, Obama tried again—an Executive Order that is much milder than Clinton's. His order would just require contractors to disclose violations of twelve separate federal labor, wage, and civil rights laws in the past three years. Contractors with repeated or egregious violations could be excluded or at least receive lesser consideration.

But good as it is, this is still a long, long way from prodding respectable companies to deal with unions or raise wages. So let me suggest a different and bolder approach. "Look," the president could say, "I won't have a hard-and-fast rule, but other things being equal, I want our agencies to do business with companies that are run democratically and put their money in real job training—and in particular we will give preference to companies that let employees elect one or more directors to their boards."

First, unlike the Clinton order, this one is too nebulous to strike down. It's just a policy, "other things being equal." Sure, by five to four, the Supreme Court could say it's illegal, but even if it does, anyone bidding on a federal contract knows it may get a boost by having employees fill two or three slots on the board.

Second, even under the bleakest interpretation of *Chamber of Commerce v. Reich*, this kind of executive order is not illegal. It's just collective bargaining that the president can't touch, because *that's* under the total control of the NLRB. But *this* executive order has nothing to do with collective bargaining because it says nothing about unions. It's about the corporate structure. It's about giving a nod to a contractor that gives a privileged position to its employees. And how does that help "efficiency" and "economy"? Well, it's enough if the president thinks that it leads to a higher-skilled workforce, i.e., better quality.

The point is: if the executive order keeps clear of collective bargaining, then under *Chamber of Commerce* it should be none of the Court's business what the president thinks.

Besides, no contractor has to comply. No one has to put employees on the board. But sooner or later, someone will try. There's too much money at stake. Some contractor will say: we let employees elect some of the directors to our board.

If one contractor does it, then another, and then a hundred others: this new model becomes part of the public debate.

How does it help labor? Oh come on, let's not kid ourselves. Any kind of corporate democracy, or any kind of worker power, is going to be a boon to labor, one way or the other, sooner or later. Bob King, the president of the UAW, is already arguing for some European-type co-determination. It's easy to imagine at least a few others who would join him.

It also helps labor by linking labor's cause with that of real corporate reform: we don't need more disclosure as in Dodd-Frank. We need more checks and balances in the companies themselves.

Best of all, it helps the Democrats to talk about labor without using the word "labor" or, even worse, the word "union." As we know, most Democrats just won't say, outside of a union hall, "You ought to join a union." Yes, of course I think they should say it, but they won't. So let's deal with it. Like it or not, the word "union" brings up too many mixed feelings. I hope one day we can detoxify the word. In the meantime, it may be easier for a president to push to give all of us a bigger say at work.

So without waiting for an act of Congress, there are ways a Democratic president could make a start in bringing back a labor movement. The big problem here is not that it might upset Congress or face challenges in the courts; the big problem is to get the public policy types to believe in it and to make it work. That's just as true for younger mandarins as it is for the boomers. The problem is to win their hearts and minds—to get the party's elite to identify with the cause of labor as the New Dealers once did.

If not their hearts, we ought to win their minds. Bank tellers now make just $10 an hour. How can that go on? At Starbucks they do better. And those are the college jobs. How else do we govern the country? Forget the welfare state. There's no welfare state that can make up for that kind of inequality. What about the economy? Purchasing power is dropping. Even the Heritage Foundation says that in the new jobs we're creating, people aren't making enough money. Yes, even the Heritage Foundation is alarmed! Its remedy is not to raise wages but to cut taxes. These people want to scrap the government. So if only out of self-preservation, the people at the top of government should start identifying with labor.

Let's just stick here with the economic peril. There's no other way to shore up the purchasing power of the country. There's no other way to effectively manage our economy. We have to bring back a labor movement.

Aren't we supposed to be Keynesians? Then I would like to make a case that bringing back a labor movement is what Keynes himself would do.

# 6

# What Keynes Would Do

If only as an instrument of economic policy, we need a labor movement, just as we need a banking system or a central government for monetary or fiscal policy. In particular, we need such an "instrument" to deal with the economy's biggest problems: our inequality at home and our indebtedness abroad. We need a labor movement to get the country out of debt, and I mean every kind of debt: our personal debt, our fiscal debt, and the trade or external debt we run up every year. Without a labor movement, we can't get out of debt.

In recent years, the big debate has been between "stimulus" and "austerity," spending more or cutting back. I was and am for "stimulus"—to do what Keynes would do. But is that all that Keynes would do? We call ourselves Keynesians, but we fail to grasp what Keynes himself might have done in our place. If we went back and consulted the sacred scriptures, the writings of Keynes himself—including the great classic *The General Theory of Employment, Interest, and Money* (1936)—we would find out that Keynes would do a lot more than prime the pump.

Here are two of the big lessons we can take from *The General*

*Theory*—lessons that also explain why deficit spending in itself, while crucial, is not enough to save us.

First, Keynes made us aware that labor markets don't work. Labor markets get wages wrong. *The General Theory* is a direct attack on classical economists who thought otherwise. Indeed, the case for deficit spending is based on the premise that labor markets get wages wrong.

It's amazing that after *The General Theory* came out, even liberal economists assume that labor markets are accurately measuring skill level, education, or talent. They don't. There's always an arbitrary element at work. Wages can be too low; they can be too high.

It's a problem of political economy. It's a problem with our institutions. We have Keynes's permission to fix it.

To be sure, *The General Theory* is not a tract in favor of a labor movement. That was not his style, and there were plenty of others in the 1930s writing those tracts. But its long critique of the labor market of classical theory is at least consistent with the pro-union tilt of the New Deal. Indeed, that tilt turned out to be necessary to get the priming of the pump to work. That is, Keynesianism—when it finally came, in the form of massive World War II spending—may have ended the Great Depression, as the New Deal itself did not. But labor law reform ensured that the Depression did not resume in 1946. We did not revive our 1929 Hoover economic model, with the kind of inequality we see today, in 2014. Keynesian-type spending in World War II may have ended the Depression, but it was the New Deal as a whole that ended it for good. The Roosevelt adminstration did create an economy built to last, as the Obama administration will not.

Second, Keynes would be telling us that we need new institutional arrangements to get us out of debt: not just personal debt, or government debt, but most and above all our trade or external debt. *The General Theory* is a tract about staying out of debt.

But while we may think of it as "external" debt, it really turns out to be our own debt, my debt, your debt, the debt of the busboys in our restaurants, the debt of the people labor is supposed to represent. Yes, we can and should raise wages—but so long as we are running this massive trade deficit, all of us will be sinking deeper into debt.

*The General Theory*, at least in this reading, lets us justify a revival of a labor movement if it will do either or both of the following:

A labor movement is justified if it gets wages right—sets wages at a level that ensures enough demand to keep us all employed. I mean a wage level that does not require us to run up our Visas, borrow on our houses, or go into debt to subsist.

And it is justified if it helps bring down our trade debt—by pushing investment out of credit and financial instruments and into the production of some kind of widget that we can wrap and ship and sell abroad.

That is, in Keynes's terms, a labor movement is justified if it can get us out of debt. Remember, Keynes hated debt, contrary to what you and I are told. Indeed, so far as I can find, Keynes never told a debtor country to go deeper into debt.

Now all of this may seem astonishing: "Wait: Keynes wanted us to get out of debt? I thought Keynes was the one always pushing countries *into* debt." But no, Keynes spent much of his adult life trying to get debtor countries out of debt; think of Germany in 1918 (*The Economic Consequences of the Peace*). Think of Keynes in the 1930s giving lectures on the need for national self-sufficiency. Think of him in 1945–46 trying to keep his own Great Britain out of debt. Think of Keynes rising from his deathbed in 1946 to appeal for a new monetary system so as to get every debtor country in the world out of debt. He even wanted to impose penalties on creditor countries such as the United States for running a surplus at another country's expense. He ends his great

classic *The General Theory* by ripping into free trade and saluting
what the Bourbons and Hapsburgs did: use every instrument of
state policy to run a trade surplus and never let their respective
kingdoms run a debt.

So why don't we hear more about *this* Keynes? It's because this
was the Keynes who attacked free trade. His position embarrasses
even Keynesians. He believed no country, ever, should run up any
kind of trade deficit, much less the trade deficit the United States
is now running. It's all there in *The General Theory*—the attack
on free trade, the defense of mercantilism. In *The General Theory*
he wrote, "A favorable balance, provided it is not too large, will
prove extremely stimulating; whilst an unfavorable balance may
soon produce a state of persistent depression."

Now to some, book VI, which has this attack on free trade, may
seem like an aside from the argument for deficit spending to cure
unemployment. What do the two have to do with one another?
Why are these two arguments even in the same book? But when
the trade deficit is as jaw-dropping as the U.S. trade deficit is, it
is harder to use deficit spending to push employment back up.
Indeed, that's just what we have found under Obama. I will try
to explain this below, but it's a big part of the reason the Obama
stimulus has failed. Don't blame Keynes for the failure of the
Keynesian remedies—he was quick, spot on, to see the problem
that we ignore. That's why he adds chapter 22, "Notes on the
Trade Cycle," and chapter 23, "Notes on Mercantilism," implor-
ing us to bring down the trade deficit. Of course, at the time the
book came out, there was no reason for Americans to pay much
attention. During Keynes's lifetime, the United States was the
biggest creditor country in the history of the world. So he never
worried about our being a debtor country. After all, at the end of
his life, he was begging the United States to get *other* countries
out of debt. If he could come back, he'd be aghast to see our

country, of all countries, becoming the biggest debtor nation in the history of the world.

"So Keynes wouldn't be in favor of running a deficit?"

Of course Keynes would be in favor of running a deficit! Even a Keynesian remedy that has lost some of its punch, as I try to explain below, is better than doing nothing at all. Besides, unlike Italy or Spain, we can run up a colossal deficit without paying interest through the roof. It has to do with the extent and pervasiveness of the U.S. bond market: unlike the case of Italy or Spain, or even Britain, there's no other place to go, i.e., to park one's money. It's unfair, perhaps, but life is unfair, and so we might as well take advantage of the unfairness and run the biggest deficit we can.

But even we face a long-term problem from one kind of deficit—not our personal debt, not our fiscal debt, but the debt we never discuss, our trade or external debt—that Keynes more than most Keynesians would now point to with alarm.

As long as we ignore our real structural debt—the failure of our labor markets to get us out of personal debt, our chronic failure to get rid of our trade deficit—we're reviving not just the Herbert Hoover model, but a Hoover-Reagan model, with Roaring Twenties inequality at home and Bonfire of the Vanities indebtedness abroad.

This is not an economy built to last: even if we pull it out of the ditch, it might go right over the cliff. Why bring back our economic model only to have it crack up again?

It's a question that should haunt all of us. Are we trying to resuscitate a corpse? That's the question raised in a book that was published in 2010 to a fair amount of attention: *Fault Lines: How Hidden Fractures Still Threaten the World Economy* by Raghuram G. Rajan, a professor of economics at the University of Chicago. He is also the onetime chief economist of the International Monetary Fund, and he has now left Chicago to head up India's central bank. Part of the book's appeal is the novelty of any University of Chicago economist complaining of income inequality—and I admit that's part of the fun. Not to worry: he doesn't come close to saying a word in favor of labor, though he does contribute indirectly to the case for it, whether he means to or not. His book is important for saying, from the other side, that we can try all the Keynesian spending we want, but we're just reviving the same top-down economy with the same fault lines as before. Even if we were to do all the right Keynesian things, there is no reason why we would not crack up again.

To simplify, here are the "fault lines" that Rajan sees, though he would not put them in quite my provocative left-wing way.

First, absent cheap credit, we Americans aren't able to spend enough to get us to full employment. That is, we don't have paychecks big enough to get the economy down to 4 percent unemployment.

 That means we take out second mortgages. We take out subprime loans. We run up our Visas. We borrow and borrow—and, at some point, we collapse.

Why do we have to go into so much debt to get the economy purring? The rich, or the 1 percent, have too much money. They can't spend it all. Even on their horse farms, there are only so many horses they really want to ride.

Rather than just sit on those big piles of cash, they lend that money to us: and that's how it works until we crack up.

Alan Greenspan inadvertently made this point when he said that we don't need equality of income in the United States as long as there is equality in spending. But for there to be equality in spending, you and I have to go into debt.

And that's what we do, until we hit the wall.

Second, and unlike the Great Depression, we go into debt another way: we buy too much and sell too little.

"Wait: I thought you said we aren't able to spend enough." No, *absent going into debt*, we aren't able to spend enough. We do go into debt, and we do spend too much. China makes too much and buys too little. The United States buys too much and makes too little.

In short: we need higher wages so we don't have to borrow to get the right level of aggregate demand. To stabilize the economy, we need the debt-free "stimulus" that a nice fat pay raise would provide.

But to stabilize the economy, we also need to make more and sell more, i.e., get some "stimulus" from people in other countries. Or put another way: we can't buy all *our* goods and services, and then go into debt to buy *their* goods and services. They have to buy more from us, too.

A reader might think, "I see how a labor movement can help us to *buy* more. But how does a labor movement help us to *sell* more?"

Hold that question. Let's go back to the first point, the first fault line Rajan describes—absent going into debt, we don't have wages high enough to let us spend enough to get to full employment. That's why we have to take out second mortgages in boom times: we don't get big enough paychecks to keep us all employed. Remember Henry Ford saying he paid his workers $5 a day so they could buy the cars? So think of it this way: now Henry Ford is paying us $4 a day, and we have to borrow the extra buck.

Who gives us the extra $1? We get it from the 1 percent. They *lend* us the extra "wage," and we pay it back to them on our Visa at 25 percent.

Of course I'm not being literal. After all, Henry Ford is dead. But the basic point is fair. The rich lend us the money to spend, because they've already spent enough. It's easier and safer to lend out the money to you and me than to invest it, say, in opening a new plant.

So all that lending at home has some role to play in our trade deficit. (Keynes would be quick to make that point.) If the rich are lending us money to keep up demand, that's a much better return—at 25 percent—than doing what the foolish Germans do, i.e., plowing the money into making more cars.

It is a point that Republicans like to make when Washington, D.C., goes into debt: if the Treasury borrows too much money, it "crowds out" investment that should go to Main Street. That was in the old days; now it just crowds out investment by the trading desk of JP Morgan Chase. Well, the same thing happens when consumers go into debt—it crowds out investment from the making of things into the making of loans.

It's why we're our own creditor nation. In book VI of *The General Theory*, Keynes quotes John Locke on this point: "High Interest decays Trade. The advantage from Interest is greater than the Profit from Trade."

By "High Interest"—if we can update Locke—Keynes would now point to the high returns to our financial sector. Indeed, Keynes might note that the rise in our trade deficit—which becomes serious in the Reagan era—coincides with the decline of American labor and collective bargaining. For it has led to an economy where keeping up aggregate demand depends on our ability to take out loans. In that sense, the decline of labor has favored "Interest" over "Trade."

Old-fashioned wage bargaining might have helped us be more competitive. There might have been less money going out in loans. If only by default we would have encouraged more investing in what Keynes called "the employment of labor for the construction of durable goods." And we might have sold more of such goods abroad.

That's clear enough, isn't it? We would have a smaller trade deficit, or maybe none. We would have had a stable aggregate demand. We wouldn't live from one bubble to another.

And that ties in with Professor Rajan's point: even if we think otherwise, we're likely to head back to bubble to bubble. At least for the recovery to date, he seems more or less right. Look at the student debt. Look at the stagnant wages. Yet look at the stock market from 2011 up to June 2014. The return on capital has soared. The return on labor has not—except for those who labor as CEOs.

Of course all of this will increase the temptation to "lend" and not "invest." The country will go back into debt. "Ah, but we're cured! Since the meltdown, we have come to our senses—we're not borrowing as much." Yes, consumers have cut back. That's why unemployment is at 7 percent. At the moment that I write, neither the public nor the private sector is taking on enough debt to bring down unemployment—and though officially at 6.3 percent in May 2014, that number leaves out millions who have stopped looking for work. Even so, if Rajan is right, people will have to go back to borrowing again. And there will be lenders—and that will divert investment from goods and services. That's why in this respect pumping up wages might at least indirectly tilt the economy out of loans and into goods and services we can sell abroad. That's the virtue of a wage increase. We might not only be able to *buy* more—we might also start to *make* more.

Still, it doesn't even occur to Rajan that a labor movement might raise wages. It's all set by skill or education level. To some at the Unversity of Chicago, it was only an illusion that unions in their heyday really did raise wages. Or perhaps they would concede: "Oh, as for raising wages, perhaps unions did a little once, in the 1950s and 1960s, but it was overrated, and anyway, it's all different now. We live in a blah, blah, 'new economy,' etc., etc." Well, first of all, these economists have never been able to explain the wage explosion of 1946–73 in terms of education and other factors they cite today or why we did not crack up again at the end of the war or even why the Great Depression did not resume.

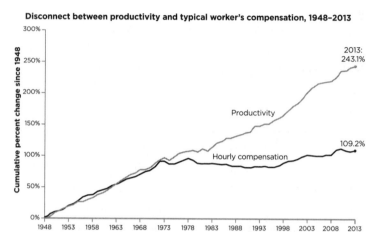

**Disconnect between productivity and typical worker's compensation, 1948–2013**

**Note:** Data are for compensation of production/non-supervisory workers in the private sector and net productivity of the total economy. "Net productivity" is the growth of output of goods and services less depreciation per hour worked.
**Source:** Economic Policy Institute analysis of unpublished Total Economy Productivity data from Bureau of Labor Statistics Labor Productivity and Costs program, wage data from the Bureau of Labor Statistics Current Employment Statistics, Bureau of Labor Statistics Employment Cost Trends, and Bureau of Economic Analysis National Income and Product Accounts.

Put another way: collective bargaining in the 1946–73 period made it possible to raise the purchasing power that kept us periodically at or near full employment. And full employment made it possible to engage in the collective bargaining that raised purchasing power.

After World War II, we had both at the same time, and we need both for any genuine increase in our standard of living. Collective bargaining by itself will not raise wages if there isn't full employment or something close to it. Likewise, full employment by itself is not enough if it is based not on collective bargaining tied to productivity but on a passing dot-com or real estate bubble—because the bubble will burst, as it did just after the end of the Clinton presidency and then again at the end of the presidency of George W. Bush.

Since Professor Rajan would put no stock in a labor movement, what would he do?

Well, he and most economists say: education, education, education. We need more college graduates. (Don't we have too many now in noncollege jobs?) Or we need better public schools. We need better teachers in the schools, or we need "merit" pay for teachers. But as Diane Ravitch, Richard Rothstein, and many other educators say, our public schools are already pretty good for middle-class kids. The problem is public education for children in deep poverty, often homeless, exposed to violence, and too rattled to learn.

At any rate, the kids in the inner city didn't cause the debt crisis, or the collapse of the middle class. It's shameful—or perhaps laughable—to pick on the test scores of poor children as the reason for the growing difference in returns to capital and labor. It's just as shameful—or laughable—to blame their parents, as some do, for the financial meltdown of 2007–8. As found by the Financial Crisis Inquiry Commission set up by Congress, the really big mortgage debt was run up not in the subprime but in the prime market, by the middle class and not the poor. When Citibank ran those ads urging people to "live richly" and "to put their homes to work," they were telling middle-class and not poor people to take out those home equity loans.

In Part Two, I would like to discuss the issue of education at more length. But "fixing the schools" is a pretty dubious way of dealing with the problem of inequality. Still, no matter how discredited, it is an idea that refuses to die. It's frustrating to me, as a labor lawyer, that there is no way to drive a stake through it. For example, a front-page story in the January 6, 2012, *New York Times* reported that "good teachers" raise test scores and thereby raise the higher lifetime earnings of the class. It's a study by Professors Raj Chetty and John Friedman of Harvard and Jonah Rockoff of Columbia. Here's what they found: "Replacing a poor teacher with an average one"—a satisfactory or better teacher—"would raise a single classroom's earnings by about $266,000, the economists estimate." Now let's leave out the methodological quibbles or the fact that we have no way of reliably evaluating good teachers. Even if it were all true, Bruce Baker, an education professor at Rutgers, offers an excellent rebuttal. As reported by Diane Ravitch on her blog, Baker wrote: "Let's break that down. It's a whole classroom of kids. Let's say . . . for rounding purposes, 26.6 kids if this is a large urban district like NYC. Let's say we're talking about earnings careers from ages 25 to 65 for a total of 40 years. So, 226,000/26.6 = $10,000 lifetime additional earnings per individual. . . . Now, per year? 10,000/40 = 250. Yep, about $250 per year."

Now let's say we try the direct approach instead and raise the wages of the worker at Aramark from $9 to $11 an hour. That's an extra $80 a week. With fifty-two weeks in a year, that works out to an extra $4,160 a year, $3,910 more than the $250 a year in the celebrated Chetty study.

And what about over a lifetime? Over forty years, the time frame of the Chetty study, that leads to an extra $166,400, compared to the $10,000 which *may* (but probably doesn't) come from a "good teacher." In comparison, the great thing about collective bargaining is that it's for real. That's real money, not the funny money of some test score effect.

So you might think that would blow away education. And Rajan, to be fair, also talks about increasing college education. But raising the percentage of college graduates from the current 30 percent to 40 percent would take *decades*, and it's not at all clear it's even possible or that it would not lower the value of a college degree.

Now there are several objections to a straight-out pay raise: for one thing, we just can't raise wages without raising productivity. But there have been *forty years* of productivity gains while real wages have fallen. It's hard to imagine how we would catch up. According to one study, if the statutory minimum wage of $7.25

an hour had gone up in line with productivity, the current law would be $19 an hour. It is, of course, much higher in other countries, with lower productivity than ours: in Australia, for example, it's $15 an hour. Seriously, are they flipping burgers any faster than we are? All over this country we could raise wages by at least $4 an hour, without coming close to breaking even with the productivity gains that should have been raising paychecks for the past thirty years or more.

And let's put aside all the discussion of education levels and productivity. What's the real economic harm in taking more from the rich? Right now they're sitting on piles of cash because the middle class isn't spending more. Fine, there's an easy fix to that. Give us some of that cash. Seriously, they aren't spending it. So why don't we? In 2013 the chairman of Stanley Black & Decker "earned" a bonus of $51.7 million. Let's lop off $4 million, which he won't even miss. That's a $2-an-hour raise for one thousand employees. Come on: what's the problem with that?

Yes, but shouldn't we leave the labor market alone? Keynes would have scoffed at that. During a recession in particular a free market is likely to set wages too low and make it impossible to provide enough aggregate demand to get back to full employment. Indeed, Keynes might say that is exactly the problem that Obama is having now. With unions gone, we have yet to provide enough stimulus to make up for the stagnant wages that are holding back demand.

The theory Keynes attacked goes as follows: If there's a recession, employers lower wages. But if they lower wages, they hire more workers. Therefore, the market will bring an automatic end to every slump or recession. Do nothing, and everything will be fine. But Keynes pointed out that if we lower wages, we lower demand. And if we lower demand, employers will not hire more workers. In other words, the labor market does *not* set the right wage, and it's foolish just to leave it alone. In *The General Theory*,

Keynes makes it clear that it is a good thing workers resist the "natural" market outcome. If so many workers had not resisted wage cuts, the Great Depression would have been worse.

Again, *The General Theory* is hardly an appeal to the Workers of the World. But it is a devastating argument that labor markets tend to get wages wrong when left alone. If the labor markets get wages wrong in terms of getting us to the right level of consumer demand, as Keynes argues, they may get wages wrong in more novel ways today. We may need higher wages, for example, to increase the demand for college, i.e., to incentivize the decision to stay out of the job market for four years, despite the debt. If we get wages wrong, then all our cheerleading for more college will be a waste of breath.

That's not an argument against more diplomas; it's an argument that, in order of priority, we should get wages right, and *then* we go for more diplomas.

Aside from all that, Keynes was a social democrat, and there is a wonderful aside in *The General Theory* that it is simply a mark of civilization for wages to go up: "Experience since the age of Solon at least, and probably, if we had the statistics, for many centuries before that, indicates what a knowledge of human nature would lead us to expect, namely, that there is a steady tendency for the wage-unit to rise over long periods of time and that it can be reduced only amidst the decay and dissolution of economic society."

If wages have fallen here, does that mean we are in the midst of "the decay and dissolution" of our "economic society"? When 22 percent of the children in the richest country of the world are in poverty, even deep poverty, one might think so.

We now have movies like *Elysium* about dystopian plutocracies, and pop culture icons like the city of Detroit. *Some* kind of "decay and dissolution" seems to be going on here. Keynes might rub his eyes in disbelief over the following from the Economic

Policy Institute: in the past forty years the U.S. average hourly wage has dropped by 8 percent, while output per worker has risen by 400 percent or more. Solon himself might gasp: it seems to violate a norm of civilization. The only parallel is the U.S economy in the 1920s, and we know how that all ended up. But this time what one might call the "Babylon effect" has gone on much longer: it may have permanently changed our character. There is more reason to worry over Keynes's famous line: "There is no surer way to corrupt a society than to cut the connection between effort and reward."

We *have* cut it—cut it not just for the traders at JP Morgan Chase or the Harvard kids clamoring to work at Goldman Sachs, but also for the virtuous middle class, who took out second mortgages. And we have no doubt cut it for the poor, some of whom have taken up meth.

Even Rajan, no prude and a free-market type, is aghast at the effect on our character. In *Fault Lines*, he titles one of his chapters "When Money Is the Measure of All Worth."

But in the end he opts for magical thinking: better schools will bring down inequality. I hesitate to scoff, since one might say the same of me: if I call for a revival of labor, isn't that magical thinking?

But let's put off that question and turn to a different fault line: the deficiency between what we buy and sell in the world. Near the end of *The General Theory*, Keynes is adamant that a country should not have any trade debt.

Now some economists, such as Paul Krugman, talk about the last part of *The General Theory*—book VI, which includes chapters titled "Notes on the Trade Cycle" and "Notes on Mercantilism"—as a kind of "dessert," i.e., something apart from his argument about deficit spending that maybe you could skip ("No, thanks, I'm dieting"). Well, "dessert" it may have been in 1936, when the United States was the biggest creditor country on the planet, but now that we're the biggest debtor we might now make it our main course.

Sometimes, while standing in line at Whole Foods—yes, reader, I admit I shop at the nonunion Whole Foods sometimes, but it's right across the street!—I pick up a copy of *The Economist*, if only to flip to the back and see the merchandise trade deficit the United States and other countries have been running the past twelve months.

In 2012 it was $540.4 billion, the biggest in the world. Last year it was "just" $471.5 billion, down because we import less oil thanks to "fracking" and the shale oil boom. But it's still the biggest in the world. Indeed, in a way, it is getting worse. Our deficit in "non oil" or manufactured goods actually rose last year by 4 percent. We're becoming less competitive in goods and services. I'm relieved the deficit has dropped, but we're still dribbling out $471.5 billion a year, mostly in lost manufacturing jobs. Consider that the entire GDP value of our manufacturing is under $2 trillion, and that imbalance is extreme. The more manufacturing jobs we lose, the more we downsize what should be the most dynamic or innovative part of the economy.

Meanwhile, while we are awash in trade debt, much of the rest of the world—including high-income countries—are in the black. How can just one high-income country be so far off course? Keynes would rip out that back page of *The Economist* and rattle it in front of us: Look!

But we don't look.

Keynes would find it hard to believe that the political class would allow the country to run the colossal trade deficit we have every year.

Many now claim that manufacturing in the United States is "back." Well, let's hold the high-fiving of each other. We may be "back" a little, but the United States is still just getting 12 percent of its GDP from manufacturing. Our rival Germany gets 25 percent. And though we pay lower wages, we just have 9 percent of our workforce in manufacturing. Meanwhile the Germans who are paying higher wages have over 24 percent of their workforce in manufacturing. It is often said over here that there are no workers in the plants. But that may be in part because like much of American business, our manufacturers are averse to hiring any employees at all.

Why was Keynes so obsessed with the trade deficit? It may be that as long as we are running a trade deficit, it is harder for Keynesian remedies put forward in *The General Theory* to work. When a country has an external deficit as big as ours, Keynesianism loses some of its punch. Consider a twist on his famous Aesop-like fable about the Bank of England, but let's replace "the Bank of England" with "the Fed." As he would put it, rather than do nothing in a slump, it would be better for the Fed to put banknotes in bottles, bury them, and pay the unemployed—like, oh, schoolteachers—to dig them up.

That's true. But Keynes did *not* say that we should put banknotes in bottles, bury them in China, and then pay Chinese workers to dig them up.

That happens to at least a partial extent when we run a $471.5 billion trade deficit with the rest of the world. Let's consider first that the point of paying the workers to dig up the bottles is the "multiplier" effect. When the Fed pays people to dig up the bottles, they have extra cash to spend. In 1936 they might have gone out to spend it at Uncle Wally's Corner Bar. The bar then hires more waitstaff. The waitstaff now go into stores and buy more Fruit Loops for the kids. Fruit Loop demand goes up, and small-time farmers in Vermont now have to buy more pickup trucks to get the Fruit Loops to the kids.

And it goes on and on, at least in a lecture in Economics 101: jobs, jobs, jobs, thanks to the multiplier.

But it's not 1936: we're not a creditor nation now, and the United States doesn't run a whopping surplus with the rest of the world; in fact, it's the very reverse. After digging up the bottles, people do not go into Uncle Wally's Corner Bar but go into Walmart or Target to buy white socks made in China. Now, thanks to U.S. deficit spending, a guy in China gets a paycheck, and *he* walks into a bar—and unfortunately the bar is in China. So while there still is a multiplier effect, it's now multiplying in China.

And that's why, in our time, Keynesianism has lost some of its punch. But don't blame Keynes. In *The General Theory* he told us not to go into debt.

He writes in chapter 10 of that book, "In an open system with foreign-trade relations, some part of the multiplier of the increased investment will accrue to the benefit of employment in foreign countries."

At any rate, though it puzzles some, it's logical why Keynes would spend the last part of *The General Theory* saying: run a trade surplus, not a deficit. In effect, he was saying: don't screw up the multiplier.

In other words, the trade deficit is just another reason why the Obama stimulus should have been bigger.

Still, let's suppose the Obama stimulus had completely worked, instead of half worked. There's still the question Rajan raises: is there any reason why the whole thing won't just crack up again?

The middle class still has no purchasing power, and there's that external debt we have with the rest of the world. That's why the debate in Washington over the deficit was so beside the point: it's what Bowles and Simpson, and the Concord Coalition, and all the rest of them can't seem to grasp. It's not that the federal government, or Washington, D.C., is in debt, but that the United States—you and me, Paul Ryan, Barack Obama, Michael Bloomberg, the Tea Party, and the homeless, all 330 million of us in this country—we're *all* in debt with respect to the outside world. It's the illusion of the Tea Party, or the Republican Party, that somehow we have to reduce the deficit so our grandchildren will not be in debt.

But in fact, if we reduce the fiscal deficit, our grandchildren will be in at least as much debt, and arguably of a worse kind.

Consider the simple mathematical truth—which of course the deficit hawks deny—that our balance of payments has to balance. And because we run a trade deficit, someone has to come up with the money to make sure it does balance.

Some readers will raise their hands: "What is the difference between the balance of trade and the balance of payments?" Yes, I'm using them interchangeably, and they're not the same thing. So let me distinguish them. The balance of payments is just an accounting statement. It's the difference between all the payments we make to foreign nations and the receipts or payments we get from foreign nations. It's not the same as the trade deficit because it counts up a lot more than goods—it counts up our foreign investments and investments by foreigners, loans, tourism. Yet all the rest evens out. Our balance of payment is out of balance because our balance of *trade* is so out of whack.

And here's the point, which seems self-evident but no one seems to get: unlike the balance of trade, the balance of *payments* has to balance.

So if there is a trade deficit—a big whopping one—then in order for the balance of payments to balance, *someone* in this country has to go into debt. Now it can be you and me—or it can be Uncle Obama.

*Someone has to go into debt.* OK, I've said it, but people keep talking as if this isn't an ironclad necessity. Let's assume the Tea Party has its way and there is no federal deficit, none, zero. Let's assume, as they say, that "we can't saddle our grandchildren with that debt."

Well, we will saddle them with debt, one way or the other, until we start selling more in the world. Either our grandchildren will be saddled with public debt as taxpayers or they will be saddled with private debt as consumers. Personally, I'd rather go into debt as a taxpayer and pay 4 percent to the U.S. Treasury than go into debt as a private consumer and pay 25 percent interest on my Visa or carry a mortgage that costs more than the value of my home. At any rate the private sector or the public sector has to go into debt.

So how can the labor movement get us out of debt?

It can do so only by creating a kind of partnership that gets the rich to invest not in loans, not in financial instruments, but, as Keynes put it, in the "employment of labor in the construction of durable goods."

We have to bring back a labor movement that not only raises wages but can get the rich to employ labor in both making and selling more things abroad. Public spending isn't enough. Traditional Keynesianism isn't enough.

Even Keynes knew it wasn't enough: that's why he turned to these structural problems at the end of *The General Theory*.

While Keynes believed in public works, to say the least—he practically invented the concept—he did not think it was the key to the economic problem. Rather, as he writes in *The General Theory*, "The weakness of the inducement to invest has been at all times the key to the economic problem."

Yes, that's why we're all in debt. We have to get the rich to invest. Specifically, we have to get the rich to invest "by employing labor on the construction of durable assets." We don't really have to get the rich to work. Who cares if they work? They can stay at home and lie in bed in silken sheets. The real point is to get them to invest—not save, not speculate in financial instruments, but invest in things, things we can sell abroad.

To Keynes, that was the mystery: how do we get the rich to invest?

It's a mystery because it seems the answer is partly structural, and partly . . . well, psychological. It's not all one or all the other. It's not just "business confidence" or "animal spirits," but "business confidence" or "animal spirits" to do the right thing, i.e., to invest in the making of a durable good and not a financial instrument.

To some extent, it's a question of politics—or at least it is an institutional problem.

I'm trying to suggest why we need a new corporate model, a stakeholder model, to do the kinds of things Keynes would want us to do. By the way, back in 1936, Keynes offered a couple of fixes of his own: bring back usury laws, penalize investment in financial instruments. He didn't like free trade: he considered himself a "mercantilist." But he didn't like tariffs either, since he believed that in the end they would do more harm than good. He was skeptical of wage cuts because they would cut demand at home—aside from offending his idea of civilization. He also disliked devaluation, which is a favorite remedy of economists on the left. But who would make the long-term investments that Keynes wanted based on what the dollar trades today?

So in our case, what structural change would Keynes make to push these kinds of investments?

Well, we don't really know because he's dead, just as he predicted we'd all be in the long run. But Keynes the acute observer, Keynes the founding father of our social democracy, would certainly be looking at the German export model, what Germany is doing today.

First, let me admit: we can't slavishly imitate Germany.

Second, we don't want to run these huge export surpluses. Keynes disliked such big surpluses, too—it was one of his grudges against the United States. But let's say we just imitate the German model enough—not to run a surplus but just to have a balance.

Indeed, if we can start improving our trade balance, that might improve Germany's own balance, which is out of whack the other way. That is, the world's biggest debtor should do what the world's biggest exporter in the developed world is doing.

Rajan is properly critical of what he calls "export-dependent" countries and what he basically regards as an obnoxious form of state-directed capitalism. He lists the institutional features that are common to these export-dependent countries. Here's what is curious: while these factors may apply to or explain China, Taiwan, Japan, and other East Asian countries, it is significant that they do not apply to Germany, though Rajan would like to make them fit.

Let's look at several on his list:

1. State corporations (or a huge interlocking directorate) that effectively plan or control investment in exports. Supposedly Germany, Inc., had that arrangement too, at least up to 1990. But it never existed in the Mittelstand, the small and medium-sized manufacturing companies that make the country so competitive. It's hard to see how it applies at all today. The big German global banks, which supposedly made this system, don't invest in manufacturing even close to the way they used to do. It's now frequently said in Germany that "Deutsche Bank is not a German bank." Instead it was buying our subprime loans or bankrolling the Greeks. As for an oligopoly, anyone can see that the EU is much stricter on antitrust violations than the free-market United States is.

2. A protected domestic market. We don't open that up to competition, because everything goes into manufacturing. Well, it's true, Germany has Sunday closing laws, and it's criticized for a sleepy domestic market. But still, the EU is borderless. Men and women from the building trades move in and out in a way that would never happen in the United States. Engineers from Spain are moving there now. Rajan notes here, defensively, that while

there is competition, Germany has watered down the EU rules. Well, that may be, but the Germans are notorious in Europe for actually following the EU rules. They are Germans, after all, and they believe, fairly or not, that while the Spanish and Italians push for broader rules, back in their own countries they don't follow them at all.

3. Use of currency controls. Yes, I admt the euro has helped Germany a lot relative to other Euro-zone countries. But the euro should have been a good deal for everybody. After all, it is more rational to make long-term investments without the currency fluctuating up and down.

What's common to most of the export-dependent economies is the strong role of the state. But what's remarkable here is that, in the case of Germany, the state is relatively weak. That means that however the Germans have done it, they have invented an export-dependent economy in which the state plays a relatively minor role.

So if state direction is not to blame, what's that leave? Only one thing makes sense.

It's the at least partial accountability of German firms—especially the "middle-sized" ones—to their own employees. If so, it may turn out that a stakeholder model like this is the only way for a country like ours to hold its own in a world of state capitalist economies. It's time to prepare. One day China and perhaps even India will pass us, just as the East Asian economic bloc will surpass the West. The United States will no longer get the free ride that comes from being the world's largest economy. One day the dollar will no longer be the so-called reserve currency that everyone has to use. One day the world may tire of our running trade deficits bigger than Italy's. When that day comes, and we have to compete, the stockholder model we have won't save us. But for us, the answer is not to turn to some form of state capitalism. The stakeholder model may be the only alternative we have, if we are to survive the rise of state capitalism globally.

Since Professor Rajan *was* at the University of Chicago, it's no surprise there is not even a single mention of co-determination in his book. And yet it is the signal difference between Germany and other export-dependent models in East Asia: the relatively powerful role of workers in running the firms. He just doesn't know what to say. And it's hard to pin down the effect, since a great deal of it may be, again, psychological and harder to trace. But the point is that institutions can put these psychological factors in play, and psychology can determine the rise and fall of economies, and even empires. The *Wall Street Journal* certainly thinks so: it is obsessed with the intangible notion of "business confidence." Keynes himself was fascinated by the notion of "animal spirits." It would be surprising if the inclusion of workers in decisions did not change the psychology of businessmen: what financial rewards they should take, what kind of options they ought to pursue, and what are the norms for letting their animal spirits loose.

The stockholder model does not guarantee the rich will part with their money or solve the "fundamental economic problem." And I am not arguing that it will appeal to investors, or even that it will necessarily survive in Germany. It may not survive. But it's the role of the state to ensure that it does, just as it is the role of the state to ensure that there is some kind of labor movement. It's in the state's interest to make sure that people do not loot the firm, or leverage it, or depart from at least one of its original functions—earning money for the country. Passing laws like Dodd-Frank or Sarbanes-Oxley for more "disclosure" does not even come close to achieving this goal. All the SEC-mandated disclosure in the world will not change the fact that there are no limits on looting, no limits on moving to the lowest-wage, lowest-skilled parts of the country, and no limits on what Bain

Capital does. We need a major change in corporate law. That requires a change in our labor law, to bring back a new kind of labor movement. And that in turn requires us to describe it all in a language of individual rights, or civil rights—which is now the only language our culture really understands.

Yes, there are scoffers. Some will scoff that the United States already is competitive. *We do make stuff.* It's true enough: we're the world's biggest manufacturer. But being technically the biggest isn't nearly good enough. Why? With a GDP of $17 trillion, and 330 million people, we have an economy that is four times the size of Japan's, China's, Germany's, and the UK's *combined*—and it should be, given our enormous head start. Yet since 1975 we have run a trade deficit every single year: not even Italy can beat that. It's great to be number one, but it's a lot better to be competing in a way that is commensurate with our size. Our inability to do so is what has been taking apart the middle class for roughly two generations.

As to our slight comeback in manufacturing, there's a perfectly good Keynesian explanation: right now, post-meltdown, consumers have cut back on debt. Even in America we sometimes pay off our credit cards. So there are fewer investment opportunities for now in debt—at the moment. So if book VI of *The General Theory* is right, one would expect that there would be a movement out of "loans" and into the production of durable goods. Sure enough, right on the Keynesian schedule, that's what seems to be happening—a slight boomlet in manufacturing. But just wait: while we Americans can make a pretense of virtue for short periods, and try to pay off our credit cards and do without, we will sooner or later be going back into debt again. As we go back again to running up our personal debts—and that will happen sooner, Keynes would say, as the federal government winds down the public debt—we will see the money tilt out of goods and back into debt again.

Finally, some will not understand this argument and claim that manufacturing by itself cannot bring down unemployment. It may be in the long run that manufacturing will play an ever smaller role in every country. But surely we can do better than 9 percent of the workforce when in Germany it is over 24 percent. And consider the lost service jobs that we incur—in sales, in advertising, in law, and, yes, in banking—when we disengage from manufacturing as much as we have.

It's true that the export-dependent models of Germany and East Asia are products of their own peculiar institutions. But what's wrong with a prudent borrowing?

But while state capitalism is out of the question, social democracy is a path we might have taken. It's perfectly logical that America *could* opt for more democracy. Is that sentimental or magical thinking? Perhaps it is—but it is much more reality-based than the premise of many Democrats that we can ignore democracy and simply fix the schools.

# PART TWO

# Democracy or Education

# 7

# Why Demoralize Our Base?

Despite all the excuses one can give, I still want to groan: "You'd think people would be in unions now, banging down the doors. Look at the plutocracy. Look at people with no savings, deep in debt, living paycheck to paycheck. OK, they elected Obama, but why don't they join unions?"

Sure, people are disengaged. Sure, they're into magical thinking: "Oh, I'll win the lottery."

Sure, those who do try to join labor get picked off and fired.

Sure, labor itself often seems inept.

But is that all?

Maybe it's because the party of the left has demoralized its base. I sometimes think that we Democrats do as much as the "top 1 percent" to tell our base the future's hopeless for most of them.

In FDR's day, it was the Democrats who offered the wild, Emerson-like, Whitman-like hope. Now even Democrats believe the grimmest Malthusian-type things:

"You can't raise wages in a global economy."

Or "Without a college degree, there's no hope for you."

Even when Barack Obama takes a swipe at the 1 percent, his only real answer is to push more of us into college. He complains that Canada and others have roared past us in the number of college graduates.

Mr. President, let it go: it's a high school nation! Why beat up your base for not having BAs? In the most recent OECD report, only 32 *percent* of Americans ages twenty-five to sixty-four had four-year college degrees or the equivalent. That means, in effect, for 68 *percent* of your constituents, you're saying there's no hope, give up: pound sand, it's over.

Let's leave out the fact that more and more of these new graduates come out of online or "for-profit" colleges. Let's leave out the fact that many of these new degrees are worthless for getting jobs. Let's leave out the fact that some of the kids are racking up $98,000 in student loans to go to four-year colleges. Let's leave out the over $1 *trillion* in total student debt—in itself bigger than the country's trade deficit, and probably half of it residing in T-bonds of some kind held in China.

Let's just put all that aside.

What about the 68 percent with no college degrees?

In the 2012 election, as you may know, Rick Santorum baited you on this very point. "Isn't Obama an elitist?" Yes, it was outrageous for Santorum to say it. Yes, it was hypocritical, too. The GOP is into Big College the way it's into Big Pharma.

But isn't he right? We *are* writing off the 68 percent.

Of course, the president is now proposing a higher minimum wage, up to $10.10 an hour; again, I do not mean to understate how important a change in his thinking this may turn out to be. Yet it may turn out to be another, subtler way to demoralize our base. It only makes starker the fact that $10.10 an hour is the party's only alternative to four years in college.

And even if we get that college-educated percentage of the country up to a full third, the vast majority of Americans of voting age will still never see a college diploma. It's no wonder that, after twenty years of Dukakis, Clinton, Gore, Kerry, and Obama telling them in effect it's too late for them and they're toast, the Democrats are in such trouble, despite the country's hatred of the GOP. Of course Obama and other Dems do not write off our base literally, but that's what they imply. "Forget it." "You're through." "College is the best ticket." "Without a college degree, you're just one of the Left Behind."

Now they may say, "Oh, we're only saying this to save the young." But what are the voters over twenty-nine to conclude? And in fact since the majority of the young will never get a degree, something many kids in the Chicago public schools know by first grade, it's hard to think of a better way to encourage high school dropouts. Why not drop out if the Democrats—their supposed champions— are effectively telling kids that a high school degree is worthless?

And by the way, what do people with BAs think when they are $55,000 in debt and have only a BA in "social media" from, oh, the Campbell College of Commerce? They must think the Democratic Party is living on another planet.

Let the GOP argue for college. Shrewdly, it never does. No, the Party of the 1 Percent sits back and smirks and lets us demoralize our base.

So can our Democratic Party leaders please shut up?

Please stop saying it is a "personal tragedy" every time a young American drops out of college.

Imagine GOP types going to NASCAR rallies and saying that it is a personal *tragedy* for every American who fails to get a college degree. That's why they get the whopping majority of the white middle class. Even if we believe it, we keep talking as if high school grads aren't even in the room with us.

Maybe they aren't in the room with us; maybe they got up and left.

It is said that in 2012 David Axelrod tried to put together a new coalition to elect Obama: blacks, Latinos, and college grads. There wasn't even a hope of getting white high school grads. It may be that black and Latino high school grads think that Democrats disdain them, too. We're just lucky they don't have anyplace but the Democrats to go.

Even President Obama's December 6, 2011, speech in Osawatomie, Kansas, his populist attack on the 1 percent, turned out to be a call for college. By the way, up to the very end, it's a brilliant speech: what a gift for the Democrats to have a president who can write! Let me say, since I knock him here, how much I like and admire Barack Obama. Go read *Dreams from My Father*: I'm surprised how few of my political junkie friends have actually read it. It's really a superb book. In his chapters about Chicago after the closings of the mills, he tells you what it's like to be dispossessed. The Barack Obama who wrote that book understands very well how we've lost the middle class.

I realize he's now the president, and he had to worry before the election how Fox, the Tea Party, CNN would twist his every sentence. Indeed, I admire the way he bulletproofs the speech. It is clever the way he uses Theodore Roosevelt—who in 1912 launched the original attack on the rich at the same town in Kansas—as a kind of human shield. It's also depressing: here's a Democrat who has to use *that* Roosevelt as cover even to come out in favor of the eight-hour day.

But after that daring proposal, he is back to "the Plan," the default "Plan," the "Plan" the Democrats have for everything: have everyone get better grades.

How do we deal with the 1 percent? It's "higher education." Literally, that's the Plan.

"We've got to up our game. . . . It starts by making education a national mission—a national mission." (There is applause.) "In this economy a higher education is the surest route to the middle class."

In fairness, I should say there is a nod to Dodd-Frank. But otherwise, it's all college. That's the Plan, the same Plan the Democrats had under Clinton, or really under every Democrat who has run for president in the last twenty years.

It's the same Plan that landed the United States with over $1 trillion in student debt and a richer plutocracy than ever.

Of course, the Democrats aren't insensitive—they want to help kids who go to college be able to file for bankruptcy to discharge their student loans. That sounds great, doesn't it? Surely even the Democrats don't believe that getting a college degree and *then* filing for bankruptcy is "the surest route to the middle class."

All right: I am being unfair.

And even if education is the surest route to the middle class, the middle class is in collapse. As we send more Americans into college the more bloated the plutocracy of the country becomes.

I could give many other examples of this single-minded focus on higher education as the way to lift all boats—except for high school grads not in the boats. For example, read the speech Obama gave at the University of Texas on August 9, 2010: "Education is not *an* economic problem. Education is *the* economic problem."

No, it isn't. *The* "economic problem" is that many new college grads come out to jobs of $17 an hour. Our employers should be raising *their* wages, everyone's—not just the fast-food workers'.

But even though he's a Democrat it's the one thing Obama can't say.

In the 2012 State of the Union—which contained not a single mention of labor unions—the president returned to his obsession with education. He had four applause lines, and I will present them as couplets.

*First couplet:*
1. "We have to stop bashing teachers!"
2. "And we have to fire more of them!"

*Second couplet:*
1. "We have to stop teaching to the test."
2. "And we need merit pay based on test scores."

OK, it's not literally what he said, but it's a fair enough summary. Even here, with the emphasis on teaching to the test and merit pay, he's pushing the need for everyone to compete with one another to get to the top. Don't we have enough of that now? Let's take teacher merit pay, touted in thousands of op-ed pieces, even (or maybe especially) by some liberals. First of all, we already *do* have merit pay for teachers. That's a big part of our problem. In no other high-income country is merit pay more out of control. Just within the greater Chicago area, one can find local school districts that pay teachers $40,000 and other local districts that pay them $150,000. Drive by exits on I-90, and property wealth varies by whopping multiples. One district can outbid the other. Those are jaw-dropping disparities for what should be geographically a single market. In this single labor market, guess who gets the best and brightest? In my state of Illinois one that spends $6,016 per student per capita or the one that spends $25,289 per student per capita? Fortunately, the answer is complicated because—against all the logic of the market (and the efforts of the rich)—some talented teachers who could make more in gilt-edged districts nonetheless opt for an inner city or other relatively poorer one. Perhaps one day, instead of increasing disparities between rich and poor school districts as a way to fix the schools, someone might actually consider *decreasing* them. Perhaps we might do what they do in Finland, or Japan, or really almost any other country and pay every teacher—I mean, *every* teacher—the same, subject to cost of living.

It does seem at times that this is how too many Democrats want to take on Wall Street: fire more teachers and push for bigger pay disparities. I read that back and blush: I'm being unfair. But the whole Plan of the Democrats is to play on our legitimate fears for our children, and that isn't really a Plan. It's a Plan for not having a Plan: and it's an excuse for not talking about giving the middle class a raise.

Or a pension, or a vacation, or even sick days.

Sure, maybe they have to talk about "higher education" to appeal to "centrists." But the problem is that the Democrats believe their own speeches. How can they "save" the middle class by pushing more into college? It's the college-educated middle class who run up much of our appalling private sector debt.

It's college grads who, during our various bubbles, are first in line to borrow the "return" that their degrees were supposed to provide—the return promised by the Democrats. Here's the fault line in the U.S. economy: between the college graduates who can access this credit and the high school graduates who can't.

In our recent economic crisis, it may be true that college grads did not take out the wildest of the subprime loans; maybe we can blame those on single mothers on welfare. But as noted in part 1, who took out the second mortgages or the home equity loans? It was the college-educated middle class. How would it help to hand out even more degrees? Do we want to create the conditions for an even bigger bubble? Here's how: let's hold down the wages of "high school jobs" so as to force more kids into college. Then let's push up college tuitions—a natural result of an artificial demand. Then let's make it easy to go into debt. Then let's make sure they don't drop out, so we end up with *more* college graduates with *more* student loan debt bidding down the pay on the *same* number of college-level jobs.

Perhaps we're not supposed to think it through. But deep down, at some level, I like to think there is some quiet place—calm, rational, reflective—in the party's political soul, whispering at night, "This doesn't make any sense."

The Republicans are supposed to engage in delusional thinking; that's their "brand." ("Cutting taxes will increase tax revenue.") The Democrats, unfairly, have gotten away with seeming to be reality-based when in fact they have their own brand of delusional thinking. It may seem to be of a more innocent kind, but, unlike the Republicans, the Democrats have been better at putting theirs into effect. That is our public policy: to hold down wages and give up any idea of increasing them through unions, while we jack up college tuitions for those who have no other place to go. Worse, millions of them go into debt, drop out, and never get the degrees at all. We have a nation within a nation of people with "some college," who turn out to be independents or swing voters, who like to hear about "education," and who may even have internalized the idea that it's all their fault: "Yes, I should have gotten better grades." But even if they buy the Democrats' message, they can still hate the Democrats for delivering it. "We'd save you all if we could, but you didn't get that degree."

And if those with "some college" resent it, even as they insist to pollsters that education is the answer, those with "no college" may resent it even more. Because the Republicans are so self-evidently delusional, the Democrats logically should be the majority party; but it's also logical that they aren't, because they push the majority away. Perhaps "insult" is too strong, but this focus on education as the response to inequality certainly leaves their supporters to work out their salvation on their own, individually, in fear and trembling, by scoring well on standardized tests and getting into the right schools.

At any rate, there's little hope of the majority of the white working class supporting the Democrats. That probably has nothing to do with people thinking that Obama or Kerry or Hillary Clinton is an elitist. Perhaps some do think that, but no one could be more personally elitist than FDR, with his cigarette holder and martinis, as well as a Harvard degree and that arch prep school accent. But, elitist or not, FDR promised to save all of us, while Obama's promise is more conditional, i.e., pregnant with the threat of damnation if we don't get good grades. It's telling that a politician with such empathy—not to mention political acumen—would keep pushing a line of argument so off-putting. Maybe it's a personal thing. Maybe it all goes back to some frustration as a community organizer. How well I can imagine the way a young Obama might have felt when he walked into those meetings (I've been in them too) with 95 percent of the crowd stupefied, mute, unable to say a word even if the organizer asks them a direct question ("So . . . what do you think about a march on city hall?"), and a tiny 5 percent who can't shut up and yammer on like idiots as he tries to talk. After all those meetings, why wouldn't the young Obama prefer the conversation of postgraduates? The problem is not that he's elitist. Or if he is, it might be a good thing. Maybe he believes that with more education, he could get that tiny 5 percent to shut up and the other 95 percent to talk. Maybe it's his daemon, the thing that urged on Socrates; maybe it's his moral purpose. Maybe something like it explains why Bill Clinton was pushing college too—as much as or more than Obama. Indeed, perhaps deep down, Bill Clinton—Yale Law grad, Rhodes scholar, and arguably our smartest president—had good reason, after too many county fairs, to think more college was the answer to all our problems.

Didn't Clinton ever have doubts, though? Newt Gingrich, after all, was a college professor—and reads a lot more books than you and I do.

Perhaps it's not elitism as such that demoralizes our base. Rather, it's the economic doctrine, the kind put forward by Professor Rajan, that education is the only way to reduce inequality.

It's the only way to raise incomes. It's the only way to compete globally.

It's not.

It's not the answer to inequality.

It's not the surest way to the middle class.

It's not the surest way to "up our game," as the president likes to say.

And educated elitists like Obama and Clinton, who travel the world, should be the first to grasp that.

As noted above, Obama is decrying a "diploma gap," which, like John Kennedy's missile gap, supposedly threatens the supremacy of our country. Formerly Number One, we have now dropped to Number Twelve (that's for adults in the age bracket from twenty-five to thirty-four). Australia has passed us. France has passed us. For that matter, *Russia* has passed us.

But let's pause here: is it Russia we're trying to catch up to?

Let's look at a country that we *should* be trying to catch up to. Germany is the biggest European country. It is not the most egalitarian, but it is more so than our own; it certainly is one of the most competitive countries in the world.

So at bars and parties I try out this puzzler: "If 32 percent of Americans between the ages of twenty-five and sixty-four have four-year college degrees, what percent of Germans do?"

"Forty?"

"That's France."

"Thirty?"

"No."

Pause. "Not *twenty*?"

Heh, heh. "Keep going."

Yes, it's just *sixteen* percent.

Those are the numbers for "tertiary-type A" education from the last OECD report, "Education at a Glance 2013."

It's true, I agree, that Germany has union-based vocational education for the people we spurn as "just" high school grads. But this isn't the same thing as our community college. Even here, in terms of what one would call "associate" degrees, Germany is still well behind us.

Of course it would be ridiculous to say that Germany is more competitive than the United States because it has a higher percent of plain old high school graduates. But it *does* have a higher percentage of high school graduates. And it *is* more competitive. The reason? It has a labor law model that tilts the country into a labor-management partnership that creates higher skills.

Indeed, there's some reason to think that if we do "up our game" and earn more diplomas without fixing our corporate model, things will only get worse. Readers who scoff should consider the 2011 report from the Pathways to Prosperity Project, out of the Harvard Graduate School of Education. The project is pushing community college as the answer—which is more plausible, but still short of the education model that we need. I will turn to that point later. But at least the report grasps that four-year higher education is not the answer; it may even be a disaster. The report notes that while the United States is expected to create 47 million jobs in the ten-year period ending in 2018, only a third of these jobs will require a bachelor's degree. And these are the new, cutting-edge jobs.

If Democrats were telling a hard truth that only college can save us, then maybe it would be all right to demoralize our high school base—all those whom the party says it can never save. If it were true, one could even admire the Democrats. "Isn't it wonderful? They don't care about the political consequences."

But it's not true. They think they're scoring points in the polls. Perhaps they are, but at the same time they're demoralizing the country. Let's put aside the effect on the college graduates, i.e., the ones at the margin, whom we're educating for jobs that will never exist.

What about the high school grads who should be the party's base?

Either they believe it or they don't.

If they *don't* believe it, at least there's hope for the party.

Oh, this group may get all steamed up and vote Republican, especially in the South. But at least they can go on thinking they could have some effect on the world, even if it's just to throw our party out of office. As lunatic as some of the GOP's hard core may be, at least they have a sense of efficacy. Unlike most high school graduates, at least they're still voting. Maybe we have a chance to win them back.

But if they *do* believe it, it's all over.

If people give up the sense that they can do something in the world, there's no hope for the Democratic Party. America's great philosopher John Dewey made a point that could apply here: once an organism loses the sense that it can affect its environment, it starts to weaken and die.

Once we convince a part of the electorate that they cannot affect the environment, then that part like any organism will start to weaken and die.

The group I have in mind will turn on not Fox News but Fox TV—and sit there for six hours a day. But that's what happens when we demoralize what *should* be our base. Some turn on Fox News and go in a rage. Others opt for Fox TV and simply tune out. Which is worse for the Democrats?

It's odd how Fox TV gets back at us, one way or the other. The other night at dinner, a friend of mine mentioned Fox. "Have you ever seen these shows?" he said.

"No."

"It's all sex. Really. And this is the conservative network, right? I ask these right-wing guys I meet: 'Hey, that's your station, right?'"

By the way, this seems to be the point Charles Murray is trying to make in his book *Coming Apart: The State of White America, 1960–2010* (2012). As a hard-core right-winger Murray would never blame Fox for the moral collapse of the white working class: he blames the liberal elite whom the Fox commentators despise. *Coming Apart* argues that in the 1960s the elite college kids had all that sex, and then spread their morals to the white working class. Then the pot-smoking kids went out to get their MBAs. It's a moral outrage that those kids became investment bankers in stable marriages, while in what used to be the moral *white* working class, there's nothing but unwed mothers, meth, and salacious shows on Fox.

To Murray, we liberals are to blame: as for the poor executives at Bravo, E!, and Fox, they have no choice but to air all that sleaze. Maybe the children of these baby boomers should go door to door and say to all the white working people who gape at the Kardashians:

"I want to apologize for all that sex my parents had in the 1960s."

They should also apologize for their parents destroying the labor movement in the 1970s and 1980s.

But Murray is wrong on his main point. The left didn't "win" the culture war; indeed, it lost the *real* culture war, the real "values" issue, i.e., whether one should be politically engaged or not. It's the left that really loses when working people disengage.

Still, is it better when they watch Fox News and go into a rage?

I think we deserve some of that rage because of the way we demoralize our base. And here's one sign it's having an effect: more and more of that rage is being directed at teachers. If education is *the* problem, as the Democrats claim, it follows that for everyone's particular disappointments in life some teacher is to blame.

A few years ago I was on a panel with a talk show host at a right-wing radio station. The idea was that left and right might find common ground on—oh, something, like better schools. And so I went, after promising, "No, no, I won't get angry tonight. Yes, yes, I'll look for common ground."

It was OK, until I hit on the Wall Street bailout. I thought that here Mr. Tea Party and I might find common ground.

Instead, he blew up: "You people on the left, you talk of putting Wall Street bankers in jail—"

(I didn't say anything about jail!)

"I'll tell you who should be in jail," he said. "It's the heads of these teacher unions."

"Put them in jail for what?" I asked.

"Put them in jail for the way they've destroyed opportunity in this country."

"Come on—how have teacher unions done that?"

He paused. "They've blocked innovations!"

"What innovations?" I asked. *Teach to the test?* But I didn't get out that last part because by now he was shouting over me:

"They're responsible for destroying lives!"

I guess this is how the right explains our inequality: it's the teachers' fault. And is it so surprising a twist on what the Democrats are saying? Indeed, to hear the Democrats talk, bad teachers are everywhere.

We don't know where, exactly, because in school district after school district, the teacher evaluation system is so important and even arbitrary. But they're out there somewhere. . . .

And that's why it's easy to imagine a young Marlon Brando, mourning:

"I . . . I could have been a contender—but I got that old Miss Grundy in the fourth grade!"

Laugh, but it's not ridiculous to some people. The political culture gives a nod to this nuttiness.

Long ago in 1920s Vienna, there were right-wing populists who blamed all the inequality on a cabal of Jewish bankers. As a Vienna wit said, such anti-Semitism was "the socialism of fools." Maybe I overstate it when I call teacher-bashing today's "populism of fools." But it's bizarre to blame our lot in life on one or two bad grade-school teachers.

Even so, the right has always had it in for teachers. In public sector unions, with all their tenure and due process rights, teachers can say just what they think. Who knows what they may be doing to turn our children into liberals? They're thinking up ways to get them to drink fluoridated water. Back in 1996, watching Bob Dole on TV give his speech to the GOP convention, I first saw how much the right disliked teachers. Here was good old Bob Dole, praising every interest group and hack association in America, until he came to the single exception of the entire evening: teacher unions. It was the only interest group he knew he could attack—and not just teacher unions, I felt, but really *teachers*, all of them, personally. At the time I was baffled: why was he so mad at teachers?

What he said that night now seems so mild.

Even the right—or maybe especially the right—feels rattled by the rise of inequality. It rattles our whole democracy; and in America, the land-of-opportunity-with-no-mobility, this rise in inequality ends up being felt as a breakdown in the relationship between democracy and education. But the crisis arises not because the schools have failed us but because the labor movement has. And if not the whole answer, the labor argument does a far less fuzzy job of explaining why so many in the middle class are in debt, or have no savings, or no pension, or why they feel they're treated with contempt at work and no one has any respect for them.

But it's easier to tell people: it's all because you didn't go to college, and if you did go to college, it's all because you didn't go to the right one.

And it is at least possible that, aside from being a distraction, aside from demoralizing our base, the promotion of college for all could make things even worse. For starters it could bloat up the already colossal student debt. But here, let me clear one point out of the way: like every reader of this book, I want more education, a lot more education, and indeed a lot more college education. I'd love to see 40 percent of adults earn college degrees. So please: don't send me any e-mails about the pleasure of reading Plato. If my 401(k) permitted, I'd go off and read Plato too. I'm for making people live at the height of their powers, as Aristotle might put it, whether they feel like doing it or not.

Strictly on political grounds, I'm for it too. Thomas Jefferson feared that without massive investments in public education, we'd live under the tyranny of the financial elite. And by the way, didn't he turn out to be right? The historian Bernard Bailyn claims: "[Jefferson's] Bill for the More General Diffusion of Knowledge is considered to be his most important contribution to the revision of Virginia laws." Jefferson did even more: he drafted the North-west Ordinance of 1787, which pushed public education and led to land grant colleges. He personally *started* a college, the University of Virginia, though to his horror it soon seemed to attract only wastrels and drunkards, like the young Edgar Allan Poe. Remember, Jefferson did all this, even though he hated government, any kind of government, with the one near-fanatical exception of public education.

Why? It was to be a check on tyranny.

Finally, there is the overwhelming economic case. I think Germany has made a mistake, actually: it has underinvested in higher education. More education *is* better than less education, since it creates a more flexible workforce. Perhaps in our education system, however, we have emphasized "flexibility" at the expense of acquiring any skills at all. But it's still a good thing.

So how can the Democrats be so wrong in pushing four-year higher education *in and of itself* without a labor movement as the salvation of the country?

First, there is a limit, even in America, to the resources we can put into education. If we divert more resources to four-year degrees for the "30 percent," we have less for the "70 percent." Let's start with just K–12, in my own city, Chicago. While we make massive investments in higher education, we've been starving K–12 in Chicago. In Illinois, there is a cap on the property tax, even as property values have shot up. The levy rate is now about half of what it was in 1994. I pay just over $2,500 for my property tax, and a younger lawyer in our office out in Oak Park is paying roughly $7,000. So in Chicago, our murder capital, parts of which are war zones, the board of education has been cutting back on social workers, mental health counselors, new instructional programs for neighborhood schools. The president is proposing more pre-K, but what about just K? Before I began representing the CTU, I just assumed there was kindergarten in all the Illinois public schools. There isn't. There really isn't a true K–12 in even some of the solvent school districts. It's literally true that many kids never get a chance to start at "K," and they drop out before they get to "12."

It's hard not to think that promoting four years of college— pushing us up from 30 percent to (say) 35 percent—would divert even more resources that should go to K–12. Indeed, the children can see it with their own eyes: even within K–12, resources are being allocated for those who go to college. Even I can see it when I take the El to work. I pass Walter Payton High, a so-called college prep or magnet school, which looks like a country club, and then pass the nonmagnet schools, which are crumbling and look like prisons (for too many of these children, school may in fact be the first stop on the way to prison). As my friend Audrey, a longtime teacher who now works at the CTU, says, "One day, I'd like to walk into a school without being able to know—just from the condition of the building—the racial makeup of the children in the classrooms." Here in Chicago, the tracking is ruthless, and it is far more permanent than in countries like Germany: unlike Germany, there is nothing, literally nothing, no serious vocational education, not even a computer program, for most of the kids left behind in the neighborhood schools. They're segregated, cordoned off.

And the kids must know they're being tracked—I mean, they aren't stupid, they can see it in the gaze, the look of the adults scanning them to see who might qualify for college—that they're going nowhere. They can see that they're in buildings that look like prisons, while brand-new schools are being built for the "good" children, especially the ones in the gentrifying class. If they get on the interstates, they can drive by and see the big glass box colleges rising up in the malls, beyond their reach. So it's no surprise that they drop out. No one has to say it explicitly, but they get the point: they've been set up to fail. Then we pretend to be upset that they keep dropping out. The Calvinists of Geneva used to have strict sumptuary laws to prohibit opulent display, for the simple reason that such an exhibition of wealth would demoralize people. Well, the higher spending on education for some and not others—and I mean the disparity in spending just *within* public education, between rich and poor school districts, and the lesser but real disparity *within* big-city districts, between selective-enrollment schools on the one hand and neighborhood schools increasingly for the very poor on the other—must have such a demoralizing effect. More than 25 *percent* of the young in this country drop out of high school without getting degrees, and the percentage is nearly 50 in big-city districts like

Chicago, where the children would have to be blind not to see they're being sorted.

It's not the U.S. college graduation rate, which is up at the top, but our high school graduation rate, which is at the bottom, that arguably makes us less competitive against other high-income countries. If we promote more college, aren't we effectively diverting resources from K–12?

Perhaps I should not use the word "diverting." Perhaps I should say we are "allocating" resources: it sounds more innocent. But if resources are limited, then pushing more college—the answer to inequality given at Osawotamie—does create more inequality, if not by "diverting" then by "allocating" more of our education dollars to those in the higher income tier who are most likely to get us from 30 to 35 percent. Does that make sense at a time when the public sector is likely to shrink both at the federal and the state level?

The same Democrats who push more college would no doubt push more community college as well. The Pathways Project claims that 30 percent of the new jobs to be added by 2018 will require associate degrees. So of course those in favor of four-year degrees will *say* that they favor more community college too. But how can a push to get us up to 35 percent with college BAs not hinder the goal of getting more people with two-year degrees? Even if we don't shrink public sector spending, we're very unlikely to increase it. So we should worry that a push for more four-year college degrees may crowd out spending for two-year degrees.

And it is at least possible this push for higher education is hurting the noncollege majority in other ways. But perhaps if we invested more in the production of goods instead of diplomas, we might not have the biggest trade deficit in the world—one that is destroying what is left of the noncollege middle class in particular.

Look, personally, I'm reluctant to think we *are* diverting too many resources into college and pumping up that deficit. I hope it's not true. But it should make us cautious about believing, as Democrats do, that pushing more college automatically makes us more "competitive" or even better off.

What's more, the push for more college also hurts some of these "extra" graduates: the ones who get the degrees but end up in noncollege jobs, like selling ties at Macy's. They're the ones for whom we divert the scarce resources. If nothing else, by having access to public credit, i.e., government loans, they have a claim on the resources that could go into more pre-K, or K–12, or community college, or something else. Yet they also divert their own scarce resources, never mind the public's, and end up through no fault of their own in a kind of debtors' mental prison. I don't need to recite the statistics.

Or maybe I do. According to an analysis published in the *Wall Street Journal* on May 16, 2014, the average student loan is now $33,000, and of course many have far higher amounts. To be sure most graduates pay off that debt—though they pay a steep price in going for years without any saving for retirement. Others go in debt without even ending up with a diploma. And in some cases even a diploma does them little good.

How so?

In 2010, the economists John Schmitt and Heather Boushey put out a study published by the Center for American Progress on the payback of a four-year degree. Their finding, based on the Current Population Survey data, is that one in five male college graduates aged twenty-five to thirty-four were earning less—less!—than the average high school graduate. That's astonishing when one considers how far the average income of high school graduates has dropped. The hourly wage for men has already dropped 8.6 percent since 1979—and now a fifth of four-year college degree holders are making less than that! Might we infer that many of those making less were what Schmitt and Boushey call "fence sitters," i.e., the ones who were unsure but were pushed into four-year degrees because our leaders keep pounding on them to do it?

How many have student loan debt over $33,000?

Journalists drool over these stories, so let's not go there. Even if there were no debt, they were still out of the job market for four years. They lost four years of at least high school job income and four years of Social Security payments. How will they make up for the four lost years (or five, or six, if they're going part-time)?

We have induced at least some people who could have been high-paid ironworkers into being low-paid tie salesmen, or insurance adjusters (or let's be really honest: the lower ranks of lawyers).

They listened to the Democrats. They have every right to turn on Fox News.

The Pathways Project is right: you can look at the projections of the Bureau of Labor Statistics and see that college-level jobs are not growing faster than noncollege jobs. There's no "there" there to justify moving our global rank in BAs for the younger generation to a higher rank than number twelve.

Yet because we need to do *something* about the inequality, that's impossible to admit. Then we'd have no plan. I know John Schmitt, who has done fine work for the Center for Economic and Policy Research, and I called him after his study came out. "Didn't everyone beat up on you?"

He shrugged it off.

"What about the argument that it still raises productivity?" I asked. "Did you see the David Leonhardt piece in the *New York*

*Times* that a waiter with a college degree is still better off than a waiter with a high school degree?" (Leonhardt's column was bashing the college bashers.)

"Look," he said, "no amount of college education will make a Starbucks worker that much more productive—in the end, he or she is still working for Starbucks."

By the way, reader, do you notice if your waiter has a college degree? I find myself thinking about this now at restaurants: "Does she or doesn't she?"

But let's take that up later, because I now bring up another question: whether it's legitimate to push for college and have the "70 percent" pay for it.

"Of course," I said, "the Democrats would say they just want to open up college for everybody."

John replied, "Let's say we push more college. Let's say we even go back to the rates of expansion we saw in the 1970s. It would still take us two or even three decades to get up to 40 percent. And even then, *what are we doing for the 60 percent?*"

Yes, what's in it for the noncollege majority who pay for it?

So I'm skeptical about more four-year college, at least as a program to fight inequality. To a labor lawyer, it seems the coward's way of avoiding what we used to call "the Labor Question." Or let me try this in a more professorial idiom: certain liberals may be right that "human capital" can balance the inequality in "financial capital," but this is possible only when human capital is deployed more democratically in the firm. That is, it is possible only if, at these higher education levels, people have more say over wages and conditions at work. Otherwise, in light of evidence to date, it seems we just end up throwing dollars toward degrees.

But it doesn't matter what I think. The student loans are out there to be snapped up, and in our kind of economy people will fight to get into college like passengers slugging each other to get in the lifeboats. Besides, if I opposed it, I'd feel the sting of

Leonhardt's column: would you deny college to your own child, even if he or she ended up waiting tables afterward? No, of course I wouldn't. Given our heart-stopping inequality, it would be heartless. On the other hand, I'm sick of hearing the case for more college in an unjust society—let me hear the case for it in a just one.

Still, if we are heading in this direction, then the Democrats have a moral obligation to offer some kind of Grand Bargain to the 60 to 70 percent who are "noncollege." That seems only fair.

At the same time, there also has to be a Grand Bargain with the 30 or 35 percent. If we want to pull in more fence sitters, as the Democrats claim they want to do, we have an obligation to make sure they can expect high-paying jobs after earning their degrees.

To put it another way, there has to be something for those left behind—a meaningful life, happiness, a pay raise—to compensate for no college, *and* there has to be something more awaiting those who push ahead. Either way, this requires not a lesser but a greater commitment to a labor movement.

Let me take up each point separately.

First, this whole project will collapse unless we revive a labor movement to raise wages for everyone.

The case for college depends on the "college premium," the gap between a college-job income and a high-school-job income. According to Schmitt and Boushey, that premium is in *negative numbers* for roughly 20 percent of the male graduates. Some graduates just above them in terms of income may feel like they're in negative numbers, given their student debt. Of course, there still is a college premium. If a revived labor movement pushes up the wages of high school graduates, then it should increase the return on a college degree as well. I understand the argument that there is no such thing as a "unified" labor market. But there still is spillover. Any increase in high school income should increase the payoff for many a college degree, even if it tends to flatten income distribution overall.

That is, if we start by raising the wages of the high school graduates, it is the single most effective way of making it easier to "increase college," i.e., increase the value of a college degree for those at the margin, whose income is just above that of high school grads. That's why countries with labor movements and more equality are beating us in numbers of college graduates. That's why we dropped from first place to number twelve. That's why Canada, the Netherlands, and Sweden are passing us. It's because we're not raising the wage of our high school grads. If we give up on *that* project, it will be paradoxically much harder to increase the number of Americans going to college. We have it backward: getting more college is not a way to increase income equality; rather, increasing income equality is a way to get more college. The flight of Obama and other Democrats away from the labor movement is misconceived because it ignores that basic point. "Might not a higher high school wage reduce the incentive to go to college?" No. On paper, to be sure, the college "premium" would drop. But that's a statistical illusion, since it's really dropping the "premium" for being Bill Gates, or even the premium for all those degree holders in the top 5 to 10 percent.

Those college grads at the bottom would still benefit. Indeed, those college grads at the margin who *are* making it are likely to be in unions: teachers, nurses, police, and even lawyers in city legal departments. Consider how much *less* college we would have without public sector unions. At the moment, it is odd how some Democratic officeholders want to curb public sector unions so we can "invest" more in education. Look at the teachers in Madison, Wisconsin: if we want more college degrees, we could do no better than to make being a teacher more attractive. Collectively bargained higher wages in the public sector explains why so many think it rational to take off those four years and go to college. In other high-income countries, more college typically goes along with a bigger public sector. That's been true from the dawn of recorded history. If ancient Sumerian rulers had not required a bureaucracy, there would have been no need for the creation of cuneiform or writing or literacy. We would still be talking on cell phones instead of texting.

But that's true in the private sector, too. The fastest-growing college job is nursing, and it's no coincidence that it's where the labor movement is strongest, too.

Second, this project will collapse if it is not seen as legitimate. Again, look at Europe. If countries take care of high school grads, they are less likely to begrudge the elite getting their perks. High school grads will subsidize more opera if the postgraduates subsidize more pensions in return. It's called "cross subsidization."

But if we're going to expand college, that's not enough to make it legitimate. Getting into college has to be fair. If we can put only 30 percent in the lifeboats, the 70 percent should know it's the *right* 30 percent.

It may be true—so the latest reports assure us—that the children of high-achieving college graduates do better than those of "low-achieving" high school graduates. Mom and Dad spend hours in the BMW with the kids going to lacrosse games and listen to Rosetta Stone for Mandarin Chinese. That's the new way that the tenured professors at elite schools explain our lack of mobility. So why isn't it true to the same extent in other countries? If it is true here, and only here, then maybe it's the very gap that demoralizes the parents who don't have access to the BMWs or the lacrosse games or the deluxe indoor swimming pools and have no sense of any control over their lives. Indeed, these people at the top tell them that, without a college education, they have no hope. If there *is* such a gap, and if pumped-up parenting *is* part of the explanation—and I doubt that we really know—another reason may be that we are demoralizing the less-well-off parents of other kids. Perhaps some study might show *that*: not a superior type of student at the top but a demoralized and dejected country below.

Just consider the falling hourly wage of adult males and the fact that the fathers have disappeared (not just African American dads but whites as well). That collapse, that demoralization, is going to play out among the kids.

Before we even *think* of more college, we need a lot more equality of opportunity. We can disagree about an increase in college but not about the increase in the opportunity to go to college. That's where David Leonhardt, John Schmitt, all of us, agree. And that requires a labor movement. That's the *only* way—because what passes for the "welfare state" actually deprives children of opportunity.

Let's start with the unequal distribution of a public good like a state's higher-education institutions. We have great state universities, open "equally" to all citizens. But look at the school districts that are supposed to be training their students for those universities: in Illinois, some pay $6,016 per year per pupil and others $25,289. Given the K–12 disparity for which a state like Illinois is ultimately responsible, how can Illinois claim to be offering a state benefit like higher education on an "equal" basis by the time students are taking the SATs?

So what's the answer? File a suit, or so say education advocates. Right: good luck with that, especially in Texas. Even in New York, or Illinois, or Ohio, it's hopeless. Lawyers like me try to define, constitutionally, a "minimum adequate education." I am in favor of such suits. I am guilty of such suits. I might even continue to try one or another of such suits. Still, even as I am drafting one, I can hear the conservatives and even relative centrists clucking, "There you go again." It's the same old liberal answer: extend the welfare state. Let's make it bigger.

What we need is a labor movement to raise the income of the parents. In one sense, the labor movement is the *alternative* to the welfare state. In another sense, it *is* the welfare state, at least as the New Dealers of long ago conceived it.

The argument here is that we need a labor movement to make an expansion of college worth it, and that applies with even more force to an expansion of community college. True, community college is just two years and cheaper, but why do it for jobs that will start at just $14 an hour?

Sure, it may still be a good idea; educators may tout it. But there is not the political will to pour in the resources if it is not a sure route to the middle class. If even four-year college is not a sure route, how much less so is community college?

That's a flaw in the case made for community college by the Pathways Project and others. In this case, however, we need a labor movement not just to push up the wages for community college–type jobs but to organize and lobby for this kind of college in the first place.

For in the old days it was hard to say where the "labor movement" ended and "community college" began. Even in my time, I think of my clients like Don Perry of Sheet Metal Workers of Local 73, who taught on the faculty of a community college. Indeed, he is Dr. Perry; he has a PhD. And both the now shuttered Washburn College and Local 73 paid him to teach. For a few years in the 1990s, I represented Local 134, International Brotherhood of Electrical Workers (IBEW), which seemed in itself to be a "community college." At least there was a joint program with contractors to provide a college-type program at Moraine Valley Community College.

It is galling to hear employers complain they cannot find skilled workers. I had a friend at city hall say, "That's what they complain to the mayor."

"Why doesn't the mayor ask them why they busted the unions that used to provide those workers?" I ask.

The case for a labor union as a "school" goes beyond these ties with community colleges. *Any* union—for example, the Brotherhood of Locomotive Engineers and Trainmen—is already a kind of "school," a way of increasing human capital. It holds people in a group. Just by being in a group, people pass on skills. Knowledge spills over. It is ironic that labor unions are disappearing just as modern economists have discovered that people learn in groups. That's why the destruction of the labor movement is an educational disaster, especially for high school grads. It removed the principal way for working people to rub shoulders with one another and pass along skills.

But that's not all.

Our education cannot end at age twenty-two. If it does, we're lost. There's a "higher" education after "higher education." I mean we need older people, mentors, old pros, to look out for us, after Mr. Chips or Ms. Chips flings us out the door. That's what the Old Labor at its best used to provide.

Think of the fence sitters described by Schmitt and Boushey. In Germany, they would jump off the fence the wrong way, at least by our standards. But these kids might end up in unions, where they would have people looking after them.

"Do you mean someone to teach them to be welders?"

No.

I mean people who would provide mentoring long after they picked up the welding degrees. In our country, what many a high school or college grad needs is a coach: someone to warn him, to take him aside, to get a kid off the couch, or maybe just to see if the coast is clear.

At this moment, there are reportedly jobs that go begging even with our high unemployment. The claim is that there is a lack of skills, and there is no doubt some truth in that. But we also have tons of young people who do have the skills but can't get past the drug tests. They screw up. There's no coach out there to say,

"Hey, son, put away the pot. Let me tell you how long it stays in your system."

More and more, there's nothing, no union hall, no place where people can go for help. We leave everything to the schools and assume that's enough.

The unions *are* schools: they make up an auxiliary system of education that we have systematically destroyed.

As a lawyer I needed mentors not just to tell me where to file a piece of paper but also to pull me out of disasters, sanctions, Attorney Registration & Disciplinary Commission charges, and the like. "Don't do that." "Tell him no." "Take that offer." Even past age twenty-five or thirty—well, OK, even forty—I needed that kind of mentoring. I needed someone to look out for me. It's as true for electricians, nurses, or guys who do tile cleaning. Community college is nice. Four-year college is nice. But that's not where we acquire skills.

Even with skills, there are thousands of ways we can go awry and be permanently, forever, gone. We shouldn't be alone out there; we should have help. That's what BMW and other German companies that come over here have tried to put in place: there is no apprenticing in this country. There is no mentoring. There is no ombudsman. There is no counselor. There is nobody to help us. Just yesterday I chatted with an officer of the Brotherhood of Locomotive Engineers and Trainmen. He had spent the weekend phoning higher-ups and corporate VPs on behalf of a member who needed to take a week off for gallbladder surgery, to head off a write-up or even a firing. Think of the 93 percent of the private sector that doesn't have this kind of help at all.

Do the oligarchs of this country grasp how much we need somebody to look out for us?

Perhaps it's different for them. Maybe it's different for sub-scribers of *The Economist*. A few years ago I picked up an issue because the cover announced "A 14 Page Report on the Future of Work." It quotes Lynda Gratton, a London Business School professor, saying that we will have to acquire "a new expertise every few years."

A new one—every few years?

That's right. She calls it "serial mastery."

And how will you and I acquire it?

Online. Alone.

But don't worry: we won't really be alone. First, according to Gratton, workers of the future will create a "'posse,' a small group of up to 15 people they can turn to when the going gets rough." Second, workers must also have a "big-ideas crowd," a different group with whom they go to "thought-provoking conferences." Finally, of course, they need a "regenerative community"—which means, I think, a wholly different group with whom to kick back after the posse goes off to water the horses.

*The Economist* gushes, "Ms Gratton's main message—that workers will have to take responsibility for their own future—makes good sense."

No, it doesn't.

We don't order up our own "posses." We don't generate our own "regenerative communities."

Yes, we need to raise wages. But we also need a labor movement to provide the education that the education system can't provide.

# 8

# What Would Dewey Do?

Still, until there is a labor movement, maybe it is up to the schools to save us. For years I scoffed at "school reformers." Don't tell me about the schools—let's change the labor laws. Those people were picking up the wrong end of the stick.

Or so I used to think, but it's not so simple.

Two centuries ago it was reasonable to believe that the best defense against tyranny or control by a financial elite was public education. Or so Thomas Jefferson believed. It was the way to frustrate the Hamiltonians, the "oligarchs." For Jefferson, the purpose of education was not to get a job—the kids already had jobs, back on the farms—but to resist the takeover of the country by those on top.

It was to teach them to be citizens: to look the oligarchs in the eye.

Well, of course, the purpose of public education *ought* to be to help kids get a job. It is to be globally competitive. See? I admit it. But why give up the goal of turning them into citizens?

Perhaps if we went back to the original goal—to teach the

young to take part in governing not just the country but their workplaces—we might even be more globally competitive.

It may sound quaint to rattle on about Jefferson or to say the purpose of public education once was to prevent a takeover by the oligarchs. To our ears, Jefferson and his fellow Republicans (still not called "Democrats") sound paranoid.

But isn't something like this happening? And here's what would shock Jefferson: the way the financial elite, the billionaires, are now investing in charter schools to replace the old public education. At the moment, the Hamiltonian elite, the Federalists, are engaged in a buyout of the Jeffersonian project.

Even we labor lawyers who scoff at school reform ought to be alarmed: the schools are being made over to be more user-friendly to a "1 percent" that puts a premium on making sure everyone goes along.

We can ignore Jefferson—he lived a long time ago—but what about John Dewey?

It's odd given our focus on education that Dewey seems to be in such eclipse. Dewey (1859–1952) was perhaps the greatest American liberal of the twentieth century. For Richard Rorty and others in academia, he is also the greatest American philosopher: our "Angelic Doctor" on the nature of experience, epistemology, and the limits of traditional metaphysics.

But he also thought in practical ways about how children learn in the schools. He thought deeply and profoundly about the problems of education. For Dewey, it had to be democratic: that is, it had to have a political dimension, the very thing it's missing now.

So if he is our greatest philosopher and if he's coincidentally the great liberal who wrote profoundly on the ways that children learn, why do we ignore what he has to say?

Well, it's not entirely our fault. He was a *terrible* writer. Though he may know what will save us, he has trouble trying to say it. Of one Dewey book, Oliver Wendell Holmes Jr. wrote, "Although . . . incredibly ill written, it seemed to me . . . as God would have spoken had He been inarticulate but keenly desirous to tell you how it was."

For the sake of this book, I have plodded through Dewey: "Come on, you know something the rest of us don't. Tell us the answer!"

Officially, Dewey is the espouser of the "child-centered" approach, which some believe has been corrupted by the kale and kombucha corners of the country into just letting children do their own thing. But he's not arguing for putting the child at the center of the world, as some of his later disciples seem to think. Rather, he is arguing for centering the child within the social and political world. In his early book *The School and Society* (1900), he writes that the goal of education is "to make each one of our schools an embryonic community life, active with the types of occupations that reflect the life of the larger society."

Even in these early books, he makes clear that schools in a democracy should teach children to act collectively—that above all children should learn to serve one another and not just try to climb over one another in standardized tests. Though I hesitate to quote a Dewey sentence, let's give this one a try: "When the school introduces and trains each child of society into membership within such a little community, saturating him with the spirit of service and providing him with the instruments of effective self direction, we shall have the deepest and best guaranty of a large society which is worthy, lovely and harmonious."

OK, this is not exactly *Pedagogy of the Oppressed*. But even more than Paulo Freire, Dewey expects the schools in a democracy to show children how to act as a community, not least in the workplace. He makes that point clear enough in *Democracy and Education* (1916). Yes, he is all for "vocational education," though not "manual training." But part of that vocation is the exercise of power, the making of decisions in the workplace. What Dewey fought was not "tracking" but the treatment of some children as princely dauphins who would go on to college and exercise power while others are to be fitted like cogs into a machine. In *Democracy and Education* he writes, "The kind of vocational education in which I am interested is not one which will adapt workers to the *existing* industrial regime. . . . The business of all who would not be educational time servers . . . is to strike for the kind of vocational education which will first *alter* the existing industrial system and *ultimately to transform it*" (emphasis mine).

Where in our K–12 is there a whiff of such thinking today?

We don't even tell children that it might be a nice thing to vote. I once asked a man who headed civic education in the Chicago public schools, "Is there any point, I mean any point in K through 12, that a teacher says to a class that we ought to vote, or it's an obligation to vote?"

"No."

Apparently not, though of course a teacher might happen to say it, on a whim.

What do they do in civic education? They have volunteer programs, but at no point is there a statement to every child that there is an obligation to vote.

If our schools today seem to ignore civics and just try to fit children into jobs, it might not be a surprise to Dewey. It was his belief that if there was no democracy in the workplace, there would be no democracy in the schools, and vice versa. His interest was not so much in pushing voting, or even formal political democracy, but in extending a democratic way of life, in *every* place, in every corner of our lives, in the schools, in the workplace, in our neighborhoods as well. Education in a democracy should above all give children the nerve to demand democracy at work. There could be no democracy in "vocational education" unless there would later be democracy at work. In *John Dewey and American Democracy* (1988), the great Dewey biography Robert Westbrook summarizes Dewey's argument as follows: the work we do must be "free," and it will not be "free" until we have "direct participation and control." Of course Dewey may not have been thinking specifically of works councils or German-type co-determination, but that's the kind of thing he had in mind. Without it, there could be no democracy in the schools.

Which comes first: democracy in the schools or democracy in the workplace? Dewey had no need to say. It was all of a piece: a democratic way of life in school, at work, every aspect of our lives. But if he is right, there cannot be real school reform until there is labor law reform as well.

That is what our single greatest American liberal once believed, but now in Washington, D.C., it seems there are few liberals who share that belief or see the connection Dewey saw between the workplace and the schools.

Given how powerless people are at work, it also might not surprise Dewey to see the current "privatization" of the public schools. Again, if there is no democracy in the workplace, it is only logical that there should be no democracy in the schools— and that there should be a "corporate" model of education, which prepares children like cogs to fit into machines and crushes out any example of what Dewey called "embryonic community life" or "spirit of service."

It's been a shock for me to read Dewey. Perhaps I've gone soft, though I still scoff at the idea that education can save us. But it may be true that if private corporations take over education, the labor movement is really through.

At any rate, even without this looming "privatization," we send kids out with so little to make their way in the world, even some of the college grads. There's no haversack, no pair of sandals: at least if we gave them a bit of political consciousness, they would have a staff for the journey.

But do we dare teach that?

It's not on the tests. There are no "metrics" that award schools for it. Why not measure schools on how many graduates in a cohort vote?

"Oh, it's impossible to measure. They don't stay in one place." In fact, I think it could be measured, but no one wants to do it.

In *Democracy and Education*, Dewey made a big point of teaching American history—to teach it as a kind of religion class, especially to those otherwise just getting vocational education. I am much taken with the idea in E.J. Dionne's book *Our Divided Political Heart* (2012) that people on the left, without shame, should be pushing American history as a kind of religion class: the religion being the "democratic way of life" for which Dewey had a near-religious attachment. To be sure, Dionne does not say "religion class" but, brought up as Catholic as Dionne was, I think I can decode well enough what he means. True, there is a powerful objection: "Then the conservative right will teach history as a 'religion class' but giving it a right-wing spin." But Dionne's answer is a good one: *The right is already teaching history as a religion class.* Our side should be doing so as well.

But if we dare to teach it, *how* do we teach it?

After all, Dewey is not for "telling" children but "showing" them, and then not just "showing" them but involving them. It seems a little strange to cite Dewey for teaching democracy as a "religion," but it was equally inconsistent for Jefferson, who opposed teaching any kind of religion, to teach democracy in the same way.

Of course I'm not against "telling" young people or making them read books like John Kennedy's *Profiles in Courage*, which I read the way young people long ago may have read Parson

Weems's *The Life of Washington*. Go ahead: tell them. We have to tell them, since it's hard to show them, as democracy in the workplace becomes increasingly rare and examples are scarce.

It's a fair question for a teacher: how do we teach democracy in the workplace if it doesn't exist?

In the old union apprenticeship programs, the kids could see it in their fathers, or their uncles, or their older brothers who did the teaching. They taught them not just about skills but about labor contracts, too. The young saw "democracy in the workplace" in the very person of the instructor. But if these programs don't exist, what's the answer?

Here's the only answer I can think of: the teacher has to be a citizen.

The teacher can set an example with his or her own life. In my own case, I saw my own teachers, Jesuit scholastics, drive up from Cincinnati to Chicago to help organize against racial blockbusting in the 1960s. That activism made a much bigger impression on me than even *Profiles in Courage*. They marched. And the Dewey who wrote *Democracy and Education* went to marches too.

And at least in the Chicago public schools, the strike helped provide a bit of this "education." It must occur to these children: "Why is my teacher in a union and my parents aren't?"

Dewey wrote long before there were teacher unions, but I think he would grasp that the best thing about collective action—and why we should be marching with teachers—is to set an example for the children.

That is the point of privatizing education. Unless teacher unions go, some kids will not fit like cogs into a machine.

Dewey's cause may seem hopeless. After *Democracy and Education*, he was in a debate with the great journalist Walter Lippmann over whether democracy had any future at all. It has always reminded me of the famous debate in 1560 between the two

Dominican friars Las Casas and Sepúlveda over whether the Indians in the New World should be treated as citizens or slaves. Of course Lippmann was not arguing that we should be slaves—he *was* a liberal, after all. But in *Public Opinion* (1922) and his other writings, he derided the idea that ordinary high school graduates could really be effective citizens. We live in a time, Lippmann wrote, when experts should decide things: like global warming, we might now say. It is absurd that people who just want to keep up with the Kardashians should be making any kinds of decisions.

Stung, Dewey countered with his own book, *The Public and Its Problems* (1927). He did believe people could make decisions. Indeed, in *Democracy and Education* he argued that the schools should prepare everyone, including hourly workers, to make decisions in the workplace, just as it should prepare them to make decisions over public affairs. Education would lead to responsibility, and responsibility would lead people to seek more education. In a sense, the test of a good education is whether it prepares us to *continue* our education—by more civic involvement, even by the reading of newspapers. With no sense of irony, Dewey, whose writing is often impenetrably esoteric, often lauded America's newspapers, while Lippmann—one of our greatest journalists— thought they were shamefully dumbed down.

Were ordinary high school (and most college) graduates capable of governing or not? Like the debate between Las Casas and Sepúlveda, there was a dispute as to who had won. Almost a century later, the warm, fuzzy part of us might put us on the side of Dewey and move on to something else (or at least that's how I feel), but the Dewey-Lippmann debate still goes on today.

And some of my heroes, like Tony Judt, come out on Lippmann's side—or at least he's not on Dewey's. Here is a fair summary of what he had to say in his last book, a dialogue with Timothy Snyder, *Thinking the Twentieth Century* (2012):

If you look at the history of nations that maximized the virtues that we associate with democracy, you notice that what came first was constitutionality, rule of law and the separation of powers. Democracy almost always came last. . . .

Democracy bears the same relationship to a well-ordered liberal society as an excessively free market does to a successful, well-regulated capitalism. Mass democracy in an age of mass media means that on the one hand, you can reveal very quickly that Bush stole the [2000] election, but on the other hand, much of the population doesn't care. He'd have been less able to steal the election in a more restricted suffrage-based, old-fashioned nineteenth-century liberal society: the relatively few people involved would have cared much more. . . . That's not an argument for going back to restricted suffrage or two classes of voters, or whatever it might be—you know, the informed or the uninformed. But it is an argument for understanding that democracy is not the solution to the problem of unfree societies.

That sounds like the Lippmann of *Public Opinion*. With fear and trembling, I still dare to say that he and Tony Judt are wrong.

To begin with, in America, we *do* have limited suffrage: limited in percentage terms that rival the voting rates in those rule-of-law paradises of the mid-nineteenth century: currently in the United States, about 40 percent of the eligible adult population *never* votes. That's two-fifths of the adult population: millions upon millions of citizens. In a 2002 report on voter turnout since 1945, the International Institute for Democracy and Electoral Assistance found that America has one of the lowest voting rates worldwide: it is number 138 out of 169 countries. If we could just reach the global norm, it is at least possible we would not have the current gridlock. We might have a majority party that could follow up on the Bain Capital commercials. If we had the "mass democracy" that Judt criticizes, we might not be in such desperate need of people like him to defend the rule of law.

In the same way, the lack of "mass democracy" is the very thing that keeps Lippmann's experts from making decisions. If we had a labor movement that pulled people in to make rational decisions in their own self-interest, we would be more likely to have the kind of government that, in the case of global warming or virtually any scientific inquiry, would let true experts have their way.

Maybe "mass democracy" would do no better. But the kind of limited democracy we do have isn't working either.

And do we really want to give up on Dewey's vision of a democratic way of life and let Big Business take over the education of the young, as the current administration seems willing enough to do?

Back in college I saw the movie *The Time Machine*, which gave me nightmares at the time and still rattles me today. The H.G. Wells hero, played by Rod Taylor, gets in a kind of golf cart and speeds off into the future where he finds only two types of people: the blond and gorgeous Eloi, who eat the kind of fruit I now find only at Whole Foods, and the blue-skinned evil Morlocks, who are deep down in the caves and are in charge of the machines. Whenever an air-raid siren goes off, the Eloi—who have no books and seemingly no opinions—go into a hypnotic trance. Then they march down into the caves, and the Morlocks boil and eat them.

For much of the movie, Rod Taylor tries to get the Eloi like Yvette Mimieux to wake up, to stop marching down to be boiled and eaten. He is aghast: why can't the Eloi pick up and read a book or at least a newspaper? *They have no opinions.* They don't even seem to care about anything as they march off to be boiled and eaten.

Once in a while, I think of the Eloi when I get on the El. At my Southport stop, the ones who get on are typically thirtysomethings—many with four-year degrees, I'd wager. Southport is nothing but gyms and boutiques; it's a perfect place for Eloi. They walk trancelike to the El. They just stare out the windows.

Sometimes I think: "They're going off to the Loop to be boiled and eaten."

Of course that's ridiculous. They're not as passive as the Eloi. They may know something is wrong. But as Dewey might tell us, nothing in their education has prepared them to resist.

# 9

# Toward the School of Social Justice

If Dewey could come back, he might be most alarmed about the education of our poor: especially minority children in big cities, where there have been large-scale experiments in education in privately run schools. For these children, we might well worry that the school as a public sphere may one day disappear.

On this point, to my dismay, I can offer some personal testimony. Somehow our tiny little firm has been entangled in litigation over schools. We have been in battles to save teacher tenure—not a popular cause. Representing teachers is as close as I have come to being an attorney for the damned. Still worse—for the last two years—we have been fighting the closing of neighborhood public schools in Chicago. In 2012 with our co-counsel Robin Potter's firm we filed suit to stop the closing of seventeen neighborhood schools—and lost. Then in 2013 we filed to stop the closing of forty-nine neighborhood schools. It was the largest single closing of public schools in the history of the United States. We lost again. Oh, we had excellent legal claims, especially as to race. But I knew there was no chance. After all, only several hundred people came up to me and said, "You're going to lose." So why take up this battle? Besides, as a labor lawyer, I'm the one saying that we focus too much on the schools.

That's the argument of the book: let's bring back collective bargaining and get on with it.

Still, two things about all these closings really gall me. First, the closings of neighborhood public schools unsettle the city's neighborhoods—especially if they're poor ones. The closings in Chicago have destabilized the city. Second, the children displaced by the closings of these neighborhood schools are nearly all African American. And I should say that in the years prior to 2013, the board of education had already closed seventy-four neighborhood public schools, and about 90 percent of these displaced children were black.

Does that look unfair? After all, only 40 percent of the children attending public schools are African American: that's right, they're not even a majority.

Now it would be one thing if the board were closing these schools to increase racial integration. As I just said, African American children are now a minority within the system. Unlike twenty years ago, there are now a lot of possibilities for integration. But after the closings the children end up in equally "all black" schools.

Actually, there are not two but three things that gall me. These closings come at least in part because our Democratic mayors—Daley and Emanuel—and so-called reformers are perfectly willing to create disruption in the neighborhoods if they can just put in more charters.

For over ten years, with no real planning, but just ad hoc, the board of education under the prodding of our mayors has created 126 new charters in a system of 680 schools. They were opening these "private" schools with taxpayer money at a time when we didn't really need any new schools at all—the student population had actually showed a slight decline.

What was the point of all these charters except privatization for its own sake?

It's certainly not to bring innovation to the curriculum. While there were glorious exceptions with the early charters, most of the ones today just hunker down and teach to the test. And do they raise test scores? No. The *Chicago Sun-Times* on April 7, 2014, ran a story under the headline "Charter Schools Show Little Difference in School Performance." Based on state test scores, even the neighborhood schools—which, unlike magnet schools, have no selective enrollment—do slightly better than the charter schools in Chicago. Many treat this as a ho-hum fact, but it's actually astonishing. The charters tend to attract children whose parents are highly motivated. And of course the charters can and do expel the kids who are behavior problems, who disrupt the schools. By all expectation, given this skewing of the student body, the charters ought to be far ahead. But the disparity in results even leaves the possibility that the charter schools are dragging students down. So what's the point of creating charters on a large scale? It seems for some schools that the only real area of innovation is to change the mix of income between teachers and managers. It's to create schools where teachers are paid $15,000 more or less, who can be fired at will, and who like most of us have no say at work. It's to turn the public school into the kind of privately run corporate environment into which most of these kids are going anyway. I assume these board members mean well—I do!—but are just more comfortable with a public school more like the top-down workplaces they know in the private sector.

At any rate, the mindless expansion of these charters has destabilized many of these old neighborhood schools. For one thing, as mentioned above, they tend to pull out children with more motivated parents (or at least children who have parents). That in itself destabilizes many schools. Resources have to be spread out even more thinly, to accommodate the addition of charters, so the neighborhood schools have to do with less. The expansion also means, inevitably, that some of these schools have to close.

And let's face facts: these neighborhoods that we destabilize were unstable to begin with. I can understand why parents want to put their children into charters, where they think they will be safe. They probably *will* be safer. I wish it were otherwise. The fact is, in the bleak parts of this city, charters can raise the draw-bridges and expel any truly dangerous children who happen to slip in. But in the end, by creating so many charters so mindlessly, we are doing even the charter students little academic good, maybe even harming them, since the charters with their selec-tivity should be doing better. So it's not worth the price we pay in destabilizing the old neighborhood schools. Let's leave aside all the other problems—for example, the fact that the privately run schools have no financial accountability, at least here in Chicago. Charters can be great in individual cases, but it is hard to imagine anyone supporting this large-scale expansion of charters if it were not going to be a form of busting teacher unions.

And there is a price to pay for all this privatization. Now there's not enough money to go around. So children in the neighborhood schools have to share books. One teacher who tried to describe to me what her school was like said, "Let's put it this way: there isn't any toilet paper."

Of course, in justifying the closings, the board never took any responsibility for its own role or even mentioned the existence of the charters. Actually, the official reasons jumped around from month to month and—during the litigation—from brief to brief. The ever-shifting justifications included: (1) the schools are fail-ing, (2) they are underpopulated, and (3) we need to concentrate resources. But reason 1 makes no sense: the "failing" schools the kids were leaving were no more "failing," or even less "failing," than the ones to which they were being sent.

And reason 2 does not hold up either. Yes, the African American population has decreased, as I noted. Of course it has: the city tore down public housing with the stated objective of "increasing diversity," and that left African Americans with fewer places to live. But the number of students—white, black, and Latino—in the public schools has not significantly decreased. While there has been a slight decline in the total number of children in the city, there has been an *increase* in the percentage of those living here who enroll in the public schools. Student population "decline" does not explain why the board has closed more than 124 neighborhood schools and displaced tens of thousands of African American children.

And reason 3 is the most ludicrous of all. If we need to concentrate resources in fewer schools, as the board kept claiming, why is the board even now still approving and opening up new charter schools?

Perhaps I should say again here that I think charters on a smaller scale can be a good thing. Even Dewey might have been in favor of them. After all, his Lab Schools at the University of Chicago were a kind of charter. One can go back and read other education reformers like Paul Goodman or Edgar Z. Friedenberg writing in the 1960s: they were looking for something like charters to get rid of the stifling regimen of public school bureaucracy and—yes—the opposition of teacher unions. And there are charters today that serve goals of which Dewey, Goodman, and Friedenberg would approve, that find new and innovative ways of connecting learning to the outside world. For example, there are charters that are partners with community colleges. It is easy to think of ways that charters could pioneer new types of vocational education. If that's the kind of charter we're discussing, we arguably do need more of them.

But that's not what we're discussing here. Rather, it's the creation of two competing school systems within a single city.

Just as none of us can love both God and Mammon, no board

of education can serve both the public and the privately run systems: it will end up loving the one and hating the other. Or to put it in less religious, Darwinian terms, one will end up depriving the other of money. And the outcome will not depend on the academic merits of the two systems. It will depend on which one has the political clout to clobber the other to death.

But let's put all of that aside. One thing seems clear to me:

These children—the children of the poor—do not need more instability in their lives. And that's exactly what these two competing school systems are bringing.

At first I thought that this was a new fight, in our day: to keep the neighborhood school as a democratic public sphere at least to some extent. Let me put it in historical terms. In the old days, in the 1950s and 1960s, the fight was for the racial integration of the schools. That fight is over, and my side certainly lost. Then the fight in the 1970s was over better or equal funding of the public schools: some still continue that fight, but that one is also lost.

Now it's a new fight: to stop privatization. At first I thought this one could be won because it is not literally about race. But now I think it will be lost because this fight too is really about race.

Let me tell you about Sherise McDaniel. She was our lead plaintiff in the suit we filed to stop the fifty-four school closings last summer.

One day she found out her son's school—George Manierre Elementary School—was one of the schools that the board was about to close. (She found out only because her son brought home a note from school.) Manierre is what one might call an all-black school, over 98 percent African American, and isn't far from a predominantly white gentrifying area. In fact, it's near wealthy Lincoln Park, where the mostly white schools are deemed "overcrowded" and bursting with kids. At the same time nearby Manierre was being closed because it was deemed "underutilized."

Now, thanks to a few lucky federal and state grants, the Manierre building is pretty nice. While the kids may be black and mostly poor, Sherise liked it: it was safe, and it had done wonders for her second-grade son, who was enrolled in special education. He had stopped talking at age two, when his father had suddenly been killed, but Manierre had been good for him; he was doing much better.

Ah, why close it?

If it was really underutilized—and that was debatable—the board could just move the attendance boundary lines. Then the school could take in more children. In this case, for example, there was a largely white school, Lincoln Elementary, that was near Manierre. Lincoln Elementary was overcrowded. Why not bring children from Lincoln Elementary over to Manierre?

Well, that didn't happen.

Manierre would close, and her son would be assigned to another all-black school, Jenner, just across a gang boundary, the designated "welcoming" or "receiving" school for those who left Manierre.

And what would happen to the building?

After we filed suit, we forced the board to turn over documents relating to the closings. One in particular, "2013 School Actions Overview," gives the master plan. Let me turn to the page describing the "Lincoln Park Planning Zone" and what would happen to Manierre. Here's how it starts:

"Lincoln Park Planning: Reduce underutilization and possibly leverage the empty Manierre building in the future."

Let me summarize the gist of the discussion that follows. The board would scoop up all the black children at Manierre and move them out to Jenner, another all-black school. Then the board would have a wonderful empty building to "leverage" in dealing with overcrowding in mostly white Lincoln Park.

In other words, Sherise's son would have to leave so white children could use the building.

Is it possible that the board felt that the black children at Manierre would be happier with the black children at Jenner? I don't think so, but I don't know. Anyway, try to imagine you were Sherise McDaniel and it was your child. It's not just that a little boy would have a much longer walk to school; he and his classmates would now have to cross five lanes of traffic, walk the long way around a gated community, and cross a vicious gang boundary to get to Jenner every day.

Sometimes people say, "Surely they can take buses." No, there are no buses, except in some cases for special ed kids. First of all, there's no money even for toilet paper, much less buses. Second, if there were buses, it might inadvertently make it easier to integrate the schools. So there are no buses. The children *walk*: two miles or so through the most boarded and beat-up and gang-heavy blocks of the city. But that's not the worst.

The worst is that Jenner is awful, not just on the other side of a gang boundary but gang-ridden itself, and it was too late for Sherise to get her son in anywhere else.

Over the years, the board always finds a way to "send them to Jenner," that is, to send black children to equally all-black schools: not 80 percent, or 90 percent, but 97 to 100 percent black. And these are not just black but *poor* black kids, in one closing school after another.

Prior to the big one last year, the board had already closed seventy-four schools, half of them in gentrifying areas near the Loop—that is, in "hot" neighborhoods such as Bronzeville and West Town. Neighborhood schools are eliminated and "selective" charter or magnet schools put in.

Well, Sherise and other parents decided to fight.

It was just too bizarre to close Manierre for "underutilization" when there were so many overcrowded, albeit largely white, schools nearby. Of course, she could guess that the board would not let Lincoln Elementary students sit in the *same* classes with Manierre students. But she hoped the board might go for what she and the parents called "the Manierre Plan."

For, thanks to Googling, the Manierre parents had come upon an astonishing fact: Lincoln Elementary was so overcrowded that it was renting space from DePaul University for the overflow, at a high price. Why not give them part of the building at Manierre instead?

It didn't have to be integration. The board could just empty out the entire top floor of Manierre and keep all the Manierre students on the ground floor. Lincoln Elementary could have the whole top floor, rent-free.

The Lincoln students would use the front entrance. The Manierre students would use the back entrance. "They wouldn't have to see our kids," Sherise said.

The Manierre parents pushed their plan at two community meetings. They argued for it to an independent hearing officer. Yet until our case went to trial, the board never bothered to respond. At the trial, after Sherise testified, the board hurriedly put on a witness to say, in effect, "Uh, well, we got the plan too late." Nonsense: the parents had raised it from the very outset, the announcement to close Manierre.

But *after* we filed suit, the board abruptly took Manierre off the list of schools to be closed.

It wasn't because the parents had protested. And it wasn't because the "independent hearing officer" said that Manierre should be spared. The *official* answer was that, oh, a lot of money had been spent on the building and it seemed such a shame to close it.

Maybe it's no accident that the board could "moot" the claim of our lead plaintiff, Sherise McDaniel. Or that Sherise was starting to get time on TV.

Of course, who am I to say? I am just the attorney.

And Sherise wanted to stay in the case. Why? "They'll just close it next year."

Under the board's own criteria, Manierre is still "underutilized." Lincoln Elementary is still "overutilized." It's still renting space from DePaul University, rather than let a single child go to Manierre. So in discovery, just before the hearing, we pressed: You're so concerned about saving money on buildings. But you have both overcrowded schools *and* underutilized schools. As our expert Woods Bowman testified, why not move the boundaries of all the schools? That saves the expense of closing fifty "old" schools and building a score of "new" ones.

We deposed the board's chief administrative officer, who makes such decisions. I quote the Q and A directly from his testimony:

Q. Why not shift the boundary lines so that some of the students in the overcrowded schools could go to Manierre and keep it off the list of underutilized schools?

A. ...A reason why not is because it is highly disruptive to relocate people from their existing schools to go to another school.

Q. But you're closing forty-nine schools, aren't you? So isn't it highly disruptive for those students?

A. It is disruptive. By definition, they're moving schools.

Any competent lawyer would have left that answer alone. Rule number one: Shut up. Let that be the record, lest he fix it on a second try. But I lost my control when he went on to say that Jenner "was a nearby school and a terrific facility that had a lot of room for Manierre kids. That was what was proposed."

As a lawyer I know better, but I had to follow up:

Q. And what was not proposed was moving any of the white
   children into Manierre to keep those Manierre children
   from the, quote, harmful effects of disruption, right?
A. We'd be going into a neighborhood and saying we're sorry
   you moved into this neighborhood to go to this school.
   You can't go to this school anymore. So that's a difficult thing to do. And so moving boundaries is a challenging thing in all communities of the city.

Ah! I was starting to argue—a bad thing for a lawyer. But at the
very end I had to get in one more dig:

Q. Did you try to use this occasion to decrease racial segregation in the Chicago public schools or foster more
   racial integration?
A. I would say *way down* our list the idea of having more
   integration was viewed as a positive. But it was not a
   specific going-in goal of what we were doing.

Wait: since I just supplied the emphasis, I can't leave that
alone.

Q. Do you think it should have been?
A. That's not for me to say.

Right—who's to say? We keep these children racially and eco-
nomically isolated, by design. But who's to say?

One night at a coffee bar in a grocery store I met Sherise McDaniel
to talk about her testimony and what the board would ask her. It's
often a lot of work to help make a witness seem natural. But it
was not so hard with her. At any rate, we had two or three meetings at the coffee bar. She was an improbable plaintiff. Of all

the clients I have ever had, she is the least shrill, and she may be the most soft-spoken, even-tempered witness for whom I've ever done a direct examination. I have no idea what she thought of me, but it's often true that a lawyer and a client start to bond because they find themselves in a bunker together. And so you find yourself saying things neither of you would say to anybody, even in your own family. So that's how it is possible that she took a deep sigh, looked away for a bit, and then said, "I often think they'd get rid of us if they could."

"You mean . . ."

"All of us."

Yes, well, I did know what she had meant.

She talked about her job helping handicapped children. "And I know I have to work harder than the others—"

She meant the other women who aren't black.

"—because there's this stereotype, I'm black, and . . ."

Of course she's wrong. Of course there's no attempt to get rid of the black middle class. And yet in a way she's right. Somehow I think, in some way I can't define, that some of this "educational" reform is just about setting certain people out of the way.

Broke or not, the board is ready to spend money—for example, building a new addition to Lincoln Elementary, a largely white school—lest we have to mix races. And by then I had come to believe that the school closings had no legitimate purpose anyway.

Close a budget hole? No, the closings were expensive and would increase this year's deficit. Concentrate resources? No, if that was the purpose, they shouldn't have opened all the charter schools and continued with plans for new ones. It took me well into the case to realize the board wanted *more* schools, not fewer. Since we lost the case, the board has approved seven new charters—and probably would have approved more, but for a howl that would have gone up all over the city.

By then of course we had lost the suit. I wondered whether our

firm should even have gotten into it. By the end I was depressed
by a whole lot of things. But if I had to single out the biggest
one, it was the feeling that by the time we put on our witnesses,
the parents had already given up. When their own aldermen did
nothing, why put any hope in the courts? But I have no doubt
about the anger; it was enormous. Closing schools was an act,
unnecessary, gratuitous, that will mark the lives of these children.
Of course some will go on and do well, maybe even get into college. But I fear that many will give up on the idea that they can
ever act together, democratically, as citizens, to make their lives
better.

By the way, we had quite a good case, even if I thought we had
just a one-in-three chance to win. We had two claims: the first
arose under a federal law, the Americans with Disabilities Act.
We claimed that under the ADA, we at least needed to *slow down*
the closings, if not stop them altogether, because there was not
enough time to prepare the students with special needs.

And there *wasn't* enough time: children with autism, for example, need months of preparation for these transitions, and the
board had no plan in place for them at all. It turned out in the
end not to matter: in the Chicago public schools, the "individual
education plans" for children with special needs are so faulty and
have so few metrics in them (to use the jargon) that we will never
know the extent to which these children were set back by having
to switch schools.

And because we had one federal claim, we had the right to
invoke the federal court's so-called supplemental jurisdiction and
bring a state law claim for race discrimination.

Some readers may ask: but doesn't the federal law prohibit race
discrimination?

Well, sort of: Title VI of the Civil Rights Act relates to schools
and prohibits both *intentional* and *disparate* racial discrimination.

"Disparate" means a government action that has a racially disparate impact and serves no legitimate purpose.

Unfortunately, thanks to a U.S. Supreme Court decision, *Alexander v. Sandoval*, ordinary citizens have no legal standing or right
to complain about such "disparate impact" discrimination in the
schools. Only the U.S. Department of Education can do so. Since
Obama's secretary of education Arne Duncan was the former
head of the Chicago public schools and an ally of Mayor Rahm
Emanuel, who was Obama's former chief of staff, there was not
much hope here. But oddly enough Illinois law does allow its citizens to bring such a "disparate impact" claim. So that's how we
got into federal court.

Why not go into state court?

We had done so for the closings the year before, when the board
was closing just four all-black schools. The judge had thrown out
the case—incredibly enough, on the ground that there was no
disparate racial impact.

I was damned if we were going into state court again.

But why not go into federal court and allege intentional race
discrimination? After all, look at the pattern fo the closings in
gentrifying areas.

Well, it was tempting, but I didn't have the nerve. Oh, I blame
it on the times. In the Jim Crow era, it was easy to allege intent.
In our time, it is often African Americans appointed by Mayors
Daley and Emanuel who end up carrying out the decisions.

At any rate, we had a good claim, at least under the Illinois law.
There was a racial impact, of course, and what legitimate purpose
was *actually* being advanced? As I stated before, the board kept
changing its rationale, and after a while none of them seemed
plausible.

Yet to get a "preliminary injunction," we also had to prove "irreparable injury" if the court did not act. And in our time, the

only injury that seems to count is how all of this might affect their scores on standardized tests.

Safety?

Stress?

The loss of all these neighborhood institutions?

It's ridiculous that no other injury counts. At any rate, the evidence based on test scores was mixed. A Rand study showed closings resulted in a longtime negative impact that the kids would never make up. But a University of Chicago study suggested that, over time, the students could get back to pretty much the same level.

But is that the real harm? Forget the test scores. What about the emotional harm to these kids?

Here's what I wanted to say in court but didn't have the nerve: "Your Honor, they're so *little*."

Yes, *little*: that's what gets me. After all, the board was closing only elementary schools; it was too dangerous to send high school kids across gang boundaries. Only small children had to walk the extra miles.

May I admit something? As a grumpy old bachelor who lives at the office, I think it had been decades since I had seen a child. At the start of the case, though, I had to go down to Morgan Elementary School to meet parents who wanted to talk to a lawyer about the closings. Since I could not find a Starbucks down there and hate leaving the Loop, I was already in a bad mood when I walked in, at 3:01, just when the bell rang, and . . . as I stood there, gaping, I saw, knee-high, running past me, laughing, running, dancing, all these little children—*little*, near the ground.

I'd no idea children in school were this small. Right then I knew: if I were a parent, I would not want my child to go into the streets and walk another two miles. It's hard to imagine the ones I saw now walking past the caged-up liquor stores I saw outside or past all the houses with big red Xs. The red X means that the house is so structurally unsound that if it catches fire, the Fire Department will let it burn.

Of course in court the board denied there would be any danger. Indeed, it has a program, "Operation Safe Passage," and signs all over the South and West Sides tell the children to walk along approved routes (and no others). Furthermore, at a cost of $7 million, the board would hire six hundred unarmed guards, who would stand under the "Operation Safe Passage" signs like scarecrows, to scare away any gunmen.

And did I say that the board hired a retired U.S. Army colonel just back from Afghanistan to supervise the mass movement of the kids, as if the whole thing were a military-type surge? The colonel said there was no reason for concern.

"If there's no reason for concern," our expert said, "why are they hiring six hundred guards?"

What about the racial stigma on the children? Preparing for the case, I happened to read the original *Brown v. Board*, the 1954 case that struck down official segregation. It took a more sophisticated view of "injury" than I might have guessed. The Court cited the research of Dr. Kenneth Clark, the great sociologist, who happened also to be African American. Clark focused not on test scores, as we would today, but on the harm to *character*, the harm from being singled out because of race. But the children in this case must *know* they have been singled out because of race: even a ten-year-old, if not a five-year-old, would know it. Rather than summarize Dr. Clark's research, I leave every reader with this challenge: go read the Supreme Court's opinion in *Brown v. Board*. Go Google it. What led the Court to throw out Jim Crow? It was the distress inflicted on these children.

I doubt that a court would even consider such evidence today. In all the lawsuits that have challenged such closings—not just

in Chicago but in other cities—some federal courts have even
mocked the idea that mere "stress" on the displaced children is
"irreparable injury." But why isn't it? Though different, it is at
least similar to the injury on which the Court relied in *Brown v.
Board*: the injury from singling out children and just piling more
stress on them because they happen to be poor and black and
their parents lack the kind of power recognized by the city. That's
why really quite little children have the misfortune to be marching, under guard, an extra two miles. Who cares about the test
scores when we look at this harm to their character?

It's the injury Paul Tough discusses all through his excellent
book *How Children Succeed* (2012). I came upon the book just
a month or so after the school closings case was over. He relies
in particular on the work of Dr. James Heckman, at the University of Chicago, who argues for early childhood intervention—
even before birth, such as tutoring expecting mothers on how to
be mothers. Heckman and others argue that poverty itself—the
deep poverty of the inner city—inflicts stress and insecurity on
children, who have no way of coping with it. To them the real
injury is the very thing that the judges brush off—the massive
amounts of disruption in their lives. The way the courts now see
it: what harm from a little stress? As research summarized by
Tough makes clear, too much stress leaves these children too distracted to learn. Too much insecurity has the same effect. Much
of the school "reform" that I see in Chicago is all about challenging tenure, closing schools, and usually removing the teachers
and staff who are some of the few adult figures the children have
learned to trust outside their families. While it may not show up
in test scores, all this stress we're inflicting will show up in how
they lead their lives. And here we come to one of the paradoxes of
*How Children Succeed*: without some sense of attachment, security, or stability, it is hard for these children to become independent actors. It is hard to acquire what Tough calls "character," or

the confidence to go out and do things in the world. In Chicago, in one upheaval after another—in destabilizing the neighborhood schools, in trying to re-create schools as union-free workplaces where people can be fired at any time—all we are doing is to increase the stress, the insecurity, in which these children live.

Much of the neoliberal project—well, let me be unfair—seems intended to bring home to the poor that they have no control over their lives. Is this really a lesson they need to learn? These children already see violence in the streets. They often see it in their homes, if they have homes. In one of the first schools we tried to save—Guggenheim, in 2012—it turned out that over one-third of the children were homeless. "Oh," my brother said, "that can't be literally true. They must just be living with an aunt or something." I was certain of that too. But when I checked with a lawyer at a homeless coalition, she set me straight: no, they are homeless in the sense that they do not know where they will sleep tomorrow night. Kids who have been rattled are being rattled even more. And that's what the board does when it throws up charter schools right next to perfectly good neighborhood schools: when it seems inexplicable, there is always political clout to explain it. Or perhaps there's another motive: to shake up the kids in these schools, put them on edge—but if Tough and others are right, these children desperately need not less but more security in their lives.

At any rate, we lost. And I'm still grieving: first and selfishly just for myself, I'm ashamed to say, since I hate to lose, but also for these children. OK, maybe test scores won't suffer. We don't know: the research is still tentative. But to Heckman and others, that's beside the point. While test scores might end up being fine, they argue that the true harm lies in a destruction of character, the kind of thing the Court in *Brown v. Board* took seriously but too few of us now do.

But while I read Tough's book with admiration—and with the

wish I'd known all this earlier—I have to part company with him in a way.

First, it bothers me the way he keeps score. "Success" in any particular child whose story is told in this book is whether the child goes off to college—and nails the BA.

So what if he or she goes to a community college or just finishes high school and becomes a first-rate welder? Then it seems the child did not "succeed."

And I have another problem with Tough's approach: the whole early-intervention thing seems so inefficient. If Heckman and others are right and if poverty inflicts too much stress on young children, it would seem simpler to raise the parent's wage. It's true: we can also hire idealistic social workers to go house to house and try to teach these distracted and often quite loving single moms how they can bond better with their children or do a better job of the "licking and grooming" that some of Tough's experts on early intervention like to discuss. But wouldn't a higher minimum wage be a better way to lower stress?

Or even better still: bringing labor unions back?

That's the case for a higher minimum wage, or a union wage, that I'd like to see Tough or Heckman make: that it helps build "character." It does so by giving the poor and the rest of us some sense of control over our lives.

Heckman argues that for every dollar spent on early childhood education, we will get back seven to eight dollars in net social welfare. Let's assume hypothetically he is right. But it may well be that for every dollar we add to a parent's take-home pay, we might get the same seven to eight dollars or even more. Some say there are more "efficient" ways to fight poverty than raising the minimum wage. But it seems at least as efficient as early child-hood intervention in cutting back the stress that is dragging down so many low-income working mothers and their kids.

———

If that's my belief, why is education now my cause?

Well, if I'm done as a labor lawyer, I have to do something. Besides I lately have done some cases for the Chicago Teachers Union. And now I find myself obsessed with preserving teacher quality—and for me that means defending what is left of tenure in the Chicago public schools.

Let me explain.

Until a few years ago I had dealt almost entirely with private sector unions: truck drivers, nurses, locomotive engineers. I knew nothing about public school teachers. For example, until we took our first case for the CTU, I just assumed it was impossible to fire a tenured teacher here.

Right? It's what my friends think.

"Yes," another CTU lawyer told me, "that's what I thought when I started—I thought it was hard to fire a teacher."

At least in Chicago—and let me stress the rules here are different—it's easy to fire a teacher, even a tenured one. Oh, to be sure, firing has to be "for cause." And the board has to hold a hearing before an arbitrator. But let's suppose the board loses.

Under state law, does the fired teacher stay put?

No—she's gone. Or at least the board is not bound by the hearing officer's decision and can fire her anyway.

Now, it's true a fired teacher can then appeal to a state court—but with no money coming in, that's a terrible burden. As a private sector lawyer I was shocked. When a stock boy at a Safeway is fired and wins the arbitration, at least the stock boy gets to go back to his job. The teacher who wins is gone. Yet people go on saying, "It's impossible to fire a teacher."

No, it isn't. But it's even easier to fire them in effect through spurious layoffs.

In the summer of 2010, when Karen Lewis and the other new CTU officers took over, the board laid off 1,289 teachers, most of them with tenure. Until then, the board had always permitted teachers to stay on for up to two years and fill vacant positions. But *these* layoffs were outright firings. Even though thousands of vacant positions existed, all of the 1,289 teachers were fired—forever, with no chance to fill vacancies and no right of recall.

Not a single layoff was for "cause." Most of the tenured teachers had excellent or superior evaluations.

Now some may wonder: "If the board has to lay off all these teachers for lack of money, how many vacancies could there be for them to fill?" Well, in a big-city school system, there are thousands; it surprised me, too. Even when the board is cutting back, it is always hiring new teachers. At the time, there were 26,000 Chicago teachers, and many retired or quit, since the job is so hard.

So why fire them outright?

Here's Ms. Price, a star teacher, teaching first grade at Alexander Hamilton. OK, the school closes. Why can't she fill that vacant position at Aaron Burr, just a pistol shot away? No, she's laid off forever, which means she's fired.

Here's what is worse: after getting rid of Ms. Price, the board will fill that vacancy with a new hire off the street. It will hire a rookie who has never taught a class.

So that began our firm's first case for the CTU. And let me tell you, I was terrified. I was a rookie too. I'd never even looked at the Illinois School Code. There is nothing to match the terror of opening that massive thing and starting to read the first page.

I knew there must be something in here we could use.

Well, one provision is clear enough: under the Illinois School Code, teachers have a "permanent appointment," based on "merit," after four years of probation. And as held by the U.S. Supreme Court on many occasions, a "permanent appointment" under state law is a "property right" that cannot be taken away by the state without the "due process" required by the Fourteenth Amendment.

So we sued. And to my surprise the district court agreed. I admit, I was flabbergasted, even though I knew our case was very strong. Usually that's not enough. Still, he was a crotchety older judge, about to retire, and because we had the stronger case, I don't think he gave a damn.

Still, it was far from over. There's nothing more painful than winning right at the start.

Now at this point some may wonder: "Why was the board doing this?" After all, we alleged that the board was free to fill the vacancies with the most-qualified teachers. And for purposes of the case, the board admitted that it was firing qualified teachers and filling vacancies with less-qualified or even possibly totally unqualified new hires.

Why would it claim the right to put in less-qualified teachers?

There's at least one perfectly good reason: to show that tenure does not matter, that qualifications do not matter. The point was to show that, notwithstanding the tenure statute and notwithstanding all the blather about getting rid of tenure to hire qualified teachers, *every* teacher is effectively an employee at will. Now the board did not make that argument expressly. But that was the upshot of its position.

What about teacher quality? That's supposed to be the concern of these corporate types who sit on the appointed boards in our big cities. So far as I can tell, it's no concern at all. Throughout the case, at the district court and appellate levels, we kept up the same argument: "Let's fill these vacant positions based on qualifications. Let's have some system, *any* system, to ensure that the kids in these schools get the best teachers."

No.

No, we don't want that.

It was impossible even to get the board to discuss settlement. The board wanted the workplace to be the same as a workplace in the private sector: if they want to bring in temporaries and build cars and Boeings down in the South, then they wanted to do it in the classrooms in Chicago, too.

In the U.S. Court of Appeals we won again, but barely, 2 to 1, and it was only temporary. On rehearing the panel wavered and decided to turn the case over to the Illinois Supreme Court to issue an advisory opinion on whether the Illinois School Code required a recall system for teachers of any kind at all.

The night before the oral argument in the Illinois Supreme Court I had nightmares. During the oral argument I tried to tell myself: "We can win." How can the court deny that the legislature wanted these poor children to have the most-qualified teachers, regardless of tenure or seniority?

Yet I knew better: it's awful when five of the seven judges look away and I cannot even make eye contact.

Still, we had a glorious dissent from two judges who said that we were right and that the children of Chicago deserved the most-qualified teachers. My friends congratulated me: "Yes, you lost, but you really got a wonderful dissent."

It galls me that this defeat—and I have nothing but defeats in school cases, as some readers may notice—passes as a victory for "teacher quality." That's the premise of the appointed boards pushing school reform: if we don't have "merit" or "qualifications," we'll get more qualified teachers. Yes, it makes no sense, but that's the claim. All we need are teachers who work at will and want to make $15,000 less a year—then we will start lifting children out of poverty! Here's the end result in Chicago—according to *Catalyst* magazine, which covers the local public schools, roughly 20 percent of the teachers are now leaving *every* year.

It is a strange thing about the neoliberal reformers: they seem to focus on low achievers only in the inner city. Why? In rural and even some surburan areas, the children are just as poor and low achieving. But in states like Illinois, the rules are often different—there are more variations—for the children in the big cities. That's certainly what struck me as I read through the Illinois School Code. For example, in every school district of Illinois, teachers have a right of recall and a right to fill vacant positions based on qualifications—except in Chicago. Teachers can bargain on student-teacher ratios—except in Chicago. Citizens can elect their school boards—except in Chicago. Federal and state courts have upheld these differences with the vague statement that the problems of the big cities are different. But no one explains why or how they are different. "There's a financial crisis." There's a financial crisis in plenty of other districts, too. "There's poverty." Of course—but not just in the cities. "There's an achievement crisis." But that's true, at least based on test scores, in other districts, too. One can find the same alleged distinctions in other states with big cities, along with the same unexplained claim that big cities are different.

What makes Chicago, or Detroit, or Cleveland, or Los Angeles, different?

Well, here's one way they are different: they have our crown jewels, the big global corporations that need protection against taxes that help only the poor.

So that would rule out *elected* school boards where poor people vote. Sure enough, as in Chicago, many big cities have boards *appointed* by the mayor instead. And the mayor appoints CEOs, as one might expect. That's clear enough in Chicago. Right now, as I write, the president of our school board is the chairman of a bank and the former CEO of the Chicago Board of Trade. The vice president is a partner at Drinker Biddle, and so on and so on.

It's no surprise that with these appointed CEOs, the property tax rate in the city is just about the lowest in the state. Here I should explain: the board is an independent unit of government, technically separate from the city. So like every other school district, it levies a property tax. "You mean there is taxation without any elected representation?" Yes: we have come a long way from 1776. At any rate, outside of the Chicago school district, in any comparable suburb or township, the rate is about 3.4 to 3.8 percent. In Chicago, it's 2.3 percent. As a result, two things are chronic:

First, there is always a financial crisis. That means more than just school closings. Worse than the lack of toilet paper is the lack of books. Even in some of the largely white schools here, the children have to share books.

Second, there are lots of charters, also run by CEO types. This isn't just in Chicago. The biggest growth in charters is in cities with appointed boards, those with the least amount of "democracy" in their systems. In Washington, D.C., 43 percent of its 45,557 students are in charters. Likewise, in Detroit, 41 percent of 113,712 students are in charters. In Cleveland, 23 to 28 percent of 40,251 students are in charters. In Chicago and New York, the percentages are smaller—14 percent of 400,545 students and 6.4 percent of 982,725 students, respectively—but Chicago has 130 charter schools, with plans to open many more, and New York has 183. All these cities have school boards appointed by their mayors.

Cities with *elected* boards have fewer charters. Atlanta, with a democratically elected board, has just 10 percent of its students in just thirteen charter schools. San Francisco has 7 percent of its 55,000 students in just eleven charters.

The odd thing is: these appointed boards seem blatantly illegal under Section 2 of the Voting Rights Act. Section 2 prohibits a state such as Illinois from any law or practice that would deny a vote to a higher percentage of minorities than it would to white citizens. So let's consider the right to elect a school board. In Illinois, there are 386 school districts, and the Illinois School Code gives 385 of them a right to an elected board. The same Illinois School Code denies the right to vote only to persons living in one district, Chicago. Take my word for it: that disenfranchises a higher percentage of the state's minority citizens in the protected class than it does white citizens who are not in a protected class. The same situation applies more or less for Michigan, Ohio, and other states, yet the U.S. Court of Appeals for the Sixth Circuit found no violation.

How?

It may seem unfathomable, but this particular court has found that there is no violation of the Voting Rights Act when the right to vote is *completely* taken away. This is not just wrong but *completely* wrong if the right to vote is taken away for some people in the state and not for others. But Illinois is in a different circuit, the Seventh. The holding in the Sixth Circuit is not binding in the Seventh or any other circuit. I admit it's crossed my mind that there could be a different result in another court. Doesn't democracy in education deserve another try?

At any rate, when there is less democracy in the workplace, there will be less democracy in the schools. It's hard to imagine the current type of school "reform" except in a country where the labor movement has collapsed and appointed boards are in control.

Still, it's not all bleak.

One day, in the middle of losing all my lawsuits, someone told me of a school I knew I had to see. What intrigued me was the name: the School of Social Justice. I wonder if even in Sweden or Finland they have a school with such a name.

Yet it is the name of a neighborhood public school here in Chicago.

Being besotted as I am with Dewey, I thought: "OK, I'm going to see it."

Let me tell you: in the daily rut I live, any kind of field trip is out of character, especially since I had to drive down to the South Side, at 7:30 in the morning, in an uncaffeinated funk, and plow my car into the permanent traffic jam known as "Little Village."

Stop sign. Stop sign. Stop sign. Little Village is largely Latino: a hundred thousand people, jammed in an area even smaller than the adjacent Cook County Jail, which runs for blocks, fencing out the good people of Little Village.

Where was this School of Social Justice? I expected to find a school not much bigger than a hot dog stand, or a Laundromat, so it was a surprise to turn left on Kostner Avenue and—

I gasped.

It looked like a Jesuit high school: a big campus with the kind of fabulous parking lot that I remember from my own high school back in Cincinnati, St. Xavier.

As it turns out the School of Social Justice is only one of four "small" schools that share this big campus and make up Little Village Lawndale High School. Luckily, at the time it was built, Bill Gates was giving out money for "small" schools. These four "small" schools, each with its own mission, together serve more than 1,400 students.

Yet one can say that, without the School of Social Justice, the Little Village Lawndale High School would not be here at all. For it was a strike, an eleven-day hunger strike by eight Latino activists, that led the board to construct this high school. As I argued above, it's best to target a strike against a Democrat. It shows strikes do work. It forced Richard M. Daley, the Democratic mayor at the time, to give in and at last build a new school *not* intended to gentrify a neighborhood after the removal of the poor. *This school was for the poor.* Incredibly, there had been no school at all in Little Village up until that time. The eight strikers started their fast on Mother's Day 2001. Eleven days later, Daley caved. At last Little Village had its school, as gleaming as the new magnet schools that appear in only the gentrifying parts of town. Yet at this moment, I envied him. How many of us will leave behind anything that will lift up generations to come or pour out blessings on the world?

A teacher I'll call Daniel met me at the door and gave a quick tour. In the atrium, there is a big Mayan calendar, with the sun lighting up today's date. Daniel said, "You can see where it's blacked out over here, in May, for these eleven days. That's when they had the strike."

Every day, every kid gets a little reminder: child, this nice place that you see came out of a strike.

Now we walked over to "Sojo," the Social Justice school, where the kids see another sign:

BORN OUT OF STRUGGLE

That's in case they miss the point.

At the end of the strike, many in Little Village said that the school should be all Latinos. "This is *our* school." But the strikers, all Latino themselves, insisted on a racial mix. The black kids come from North Lawndale, home to the poorest of the poor.

We were heading for the science lab where Daniel teaches.

"Why is it So*jo*, and not . . . ?"

"Yes, it should be So*ju*, but 'Soju' is the name of a Korean liquor."

"I bet for a lot of these kids, it's nicer than what they have at home," I said.

"You should see the pool."

I looked into the cafeteria.

"How many of the kids qualify for the free breakfast and lunch?"

"About 90 percent," he said.

The public schools have become soup kitchens, too.

In such a nice-looking building, even the poorest kids might be able to feel middle class. Like little Mayan calendars, they could reflect back the radiance of the building.

We reached the science lab. Unlike in many public schools, there are up-to-date science and computer labs. Daniel told me, "A lot of people are surprised that we even teach science."

"Right . . . at the School of Social Justice, how do you do that?"

I could see the teaching of history, or maybe even English, as a lead-in to social justice, but science . . . well, with state mandates, it has to fit in. Yet as Daniel spoke, the connection here became clearer than with history or anything else I had in mind.

"We start from things that concern these kids. For example, we have a unit where they bring in beauty products. We talk about them. We talk how Eurocentric these things are, how the ideas of beauty are slanted, or the way they objectify women. . . . Then we look at the chemicals in these products. We look at the lead in the lipstick. We look at the various aluminum combinations, what's in the moisturizers. . . ."

Good: warn the kids about the pushers before they get hooked.

"We have a consumer electronics unit. We look at the metals inside, explain the metals—look at copper wire, for example—and talk about where it came from, how it is extracted, how it is combined . . . but also talk about the mineral resource exploitation in Latin America and other countries, how it is tied to colonialism. It's to teach the science but also to connect their lived experience with these broader concerns—bring it down to things like how to dispose of their cell phones, and why."

He was ready to go on, but the kids kept popping in to ask questions. Apparently, the attendance rate here is very high.

Why *wouldn't* they come here?

Though it wasn't from Daniel, I did hear that the kids have gone out on strikes, for one cause or another. Some kids ask the teachers, "Should we do this . . . ?" The teachers blush: "We can't tell you. . . ."

Here is just a sample of the famous faces that beam down on these kids between classes from posters like blown-up baseball cards:

Mohandas Gandhi
Harold Washington

Rudy Lozano
Cesar Chavez

And there is political art:

Picasso's *Guernica*
Art Spiegelman's *Maus*

Who could leave here and not want to change the world?

The question is not whether these kids will go on to four-year colleges. If they do, fine. If they don't, that may be OK too. No, the question is whether they will bring some equilibrium to a country whose political system is cracking up. As I have argued, that is the Jeffersonian purpose of public education—the prevention of tyranny.

To be sure, Jefferson went too far. The defense of the Republic cannot be the *only* purpose. These kids do need to go out and get jobs. But is it too much to say that in 2012, in a much diluted and watered-down way, the prevention of tyranny should at least be *one* of the purposes?

To some, the School of Social Justice goes too far. But consider it from a legal point of view: this may be the only school in compliance with the spirit of the Northwest Ordinance—the only one doing what Jefferson, who drafted the law, intended a school to do.

I had a question for Daniel. "Has anyone ever tried to rank the various public schools not on how well the students do on the state tests but on whether they actually vote after they graduate?"

"That would certainly be an interesting study."

"So in this school, here, what percent will vote when they get out?"

He paused. "About a third of the kids here are undocumented."

Well, so much for that study.

As I left the school, we walked past the pool: it's as big and fine as any pool in the state. I kept thinking: "This is what you get when you go out on strike." I thought the graduates of the School of Social Justice will at least carry the memory of that— the glorious natatorium that came out of the strike. That pool is no mirage, is it? It is a practical demonstration that when people act collectively anything is possible.

I wish people my age could bequeath a labor movement to the next generation the way the strikers bequeathed this school.

If we can't give them an actual labor movement, at least we could leave a blueprint. We could leave the kids a plan.

## PART THREE

# We Will Come Back— as Something New

# 10

# What King Would Do

If labor is to come back, it has to come back as something different. It can't be one more damn thing imposed on us from the outside. We get enough of that now. Labor is the one thing that can save us. But the thing that can save us is not the labor that we have now. The "old" labor, hunkering down in those big buildings in Washington, D.C., can't be the instrument of our deliverance. Yes, people want higher wages. They want pensions. From time to time, they may even want solidarity. They want much of what the old labor is set up to give. But the "new" labor, unlike the old labor, can't do it all for us. The period of childhood or tutelage—the nature of it depends on which union is the "parent"—has to come to an end. In the century to come, more individualistic than the previous one, the new labor has to step back, give up its control over the old labor law remedies, and let us do things for ourselves. That's what the Germans and their West European imitators grasp. That's why there are works councils and workers sitting in equal numbers with shareholders on the supervisory boards of huge global corporations. To be sure, the works council and the co-determined board have a strong connection with the union, but there are no union officers or business agents to make these decisions for them.

I may be too taken with the arrangements of social democratic Europe for American tastes, but this "entrepreneurial" side of, and individual initiative within, the labor movement in Europe sometimes makes it seem more like us than we actually are. No doubt I have spent too much time on mountaintops where the German unions have their spas and conference centers and seen how they train employees to be on works councils, with union officers acting only as "consultants." I feel the attraction of the call to "rank-and-file" democracy, but there is also a deeply human craving not to be just "rank" or "file" but to be someone singled out as an officeholder. How well I know from my own life that craving to hold an office! In some manner or other, we have to create more offices to hold—offices that money or power cannot buy. Whether we do it in some "American" way or in a way slavishly imitative of someone else's system, I don't really care. But I know that old labor has to release the too-tight grip it has had up to now on the labor movement at large and let individual members take on bigger roles. Right now there's a guy in Alabama who deep down is waiting for a labor movement that won't be imposed on him but one that he can pick up and put down with the same kind of control over it that he wants for his own job.

I am quite certain that, besieged as it is, labor should *not* be denied the right to an "agency shop" at this time, though: because of the structure of our labor law, especially the "duty of fair representation," losing the agency shop would be too unfair to the unions. But we might consider the day when it would be possible to give that up, because it is the biggest single reason for all the rage and howling of the Fox TV right against labor. That rage may be unfair for all sorts of reasons, but it is not hard to understand. The economist Albert O. Hirschman wrote that effective organizations must provide for their members either "exit" or "voice."

In a labor movement where rank-and-file members have no real electoral control over the top officers (no voice, in Hirschman's sense—not even a right to vote directly in many cases) and where there is no ability for individuals to opt out (no "exit"), then labor looks like one more alien thing over which people have no control. It looks that way even in the "right-to-work" states where employees do have the right to drop out, because labor's character as an alien and unresponsive "outside" thing is partly shaped by Section 9(a) of the NLRA. That's the section that allows for "exclusive representation."

Even in a right-to-work state, where members can opt out of paying dues, no one can opt out of a system that makes a labor union his or her "exclusive representative." However one feels about the principle of exclusive representation, the fact that it survives in the hyperatomized United States but in virtually no other country is one of the stranger things I know. But thanks to right-to-work laws, what should be a boon to labor becomes a growing financial drag: for even in the twenty-four states that have right-to-work laws, a labor union with a certification under Section 9(a) has a legal duty to represent every single employee— equally, fairly, and for free and without charge. Yes, it's a legal duty to help everyone, for free, no matter how extreme a union-busting Tea Party person that may be.

Given that duty, it is just wrong to saddle labor with a federal right-to-work law, which lets anyone who likes be a free rider. As a matter of fairness, if the agency shop goes, exclusive representation must have to go. That may have been what gave pause to some of the conservative justices in *Harris v. Quinn*: "Maybe if we get rid of the agency shop, the whole model has to go." And maybe some people in the Chamber of Commerce *like* the current model. It would be especially unfair to get rid of the agency shop when unions in America do *not* have works councils of the German kind—because in Germany, it is not the union but the employer which pays for a works council that represents every-one. A right-to-work law is also unfair while Americans lack an effective right to join a union, freely and fairly, without being fired. That right would expand the pool of Americans who might voluntarily contribute to keep a labor movement going.

So how do we change things?

## 1. Make It a Civil Right to Join a Union

Of course, there has to be an *effective* right to join a union in the first place, freely and fairly, without being fired. It is even more urgent as right-to-work laws spread. It's a matter of fairness to labor. It is the only thing that can save us.

How can we put in place such a right? In our day, which we can no longer speak of as being even "post"–New Deal, there is just one and only one way left: namely, not to bother with the Wagner Act and other New Deal laws and instead use the Civil Rights Act of 1964, as amended and greatly strengthened in 1991, to add one more type of prohibited discrimination and stop employers from going after a Sister or Brother because he or she supports a union. Then give that Sister or Brother all the legal firepower that is available under that act. To the boilerplate ban on dis-crimination in employment for race, age, gender, handicap, and everything else on the list, we just need to add six little words: "on the basis of union membership." Six little words—in one form or another—are the only thing that can save us. Let employees who are fired just for wearing a union button bring the same legal claims that we make under existing civil rights laws. Make it a civil right to join or not to join a union. I can't think of anything that would do more to round out the vision of Martin Luther King Jr. He may have started out as "just" a civil rights leader, but he died also as a kind of labor leader, heading up the last general strike in America—to help the garbage workers in Memphis—on the day he was shot and killed.

The case for such a civil right is set forth by Richard D. Kahlenberg and Moshe Marvit in their short and punchy Century Foundation book *Why Labor Organizing Should Be a Civil Right* (2012), to which I contributed a preface. They would amend the Civil Rights Act to outlaw the discrimination that is so crucial to union busting and has caused the unionized share of the private sector to drop to a mere 6.8 percent. To the credit of the authors, congressman Keith Ellison has just now introduced a bill to create such a legal right. Technically, the bill amends not the Civil Rights Act but the Wagner Act. Yet it comes down to the same thing—to provide the legal remedies we give to plaintiffs in civil rights suits. The claim here is not that the "civil rights revolution" has failed but that we must extend it to the most neglected civil right of all—the right to join a union.

Some may believe—or at least I have heard the claim—that we should keep our civil rights model for "identity"-type claims or that it is somehow inappropriate or even dangerous to equate the now accepted civil rights of the 1960s with a more disruptive and new civil right to join a union. But wouldn't King himself push for such a right? Consider how many speeches King gave in which he tied the civil rights movement to the labor movement or made clear that black Americans would not be free at last until all of us as a people checked the power of capital in America. Now that King has achieved a kind of sainthood, many like to gloss over his attack on capitalism—just as we don't dwell on the fact that Nelson Mandela was in the Communist Party. But the March on Washington in 1963—which helped turn King into an enduring icon—was intended as a labor event, i.e., a rally for a higher minimum wage. He also gave some of his best and most fiery speeches not just in black churches but at labor union conventions, yes, even to the AFL-CIO in Florida in 1961. After all, it was not the MacArthur Foundation but Reuther's UAW—the progressive part of the labor movement—that at crucial moments provided the funding for King. It was Reuther who put up the money to bail King out of that Birmingham jail. It is generally believed that it was King's blistering attack on U.S. capitalism at that AFL-CIO convention that first prompted J. Edgar Hoover and the FBI to consider wiretapping King's phone.

Yes, of course King would have identified the right to join a union as a civil right. Remember, labor law was not as dysfunctional as it appears today. For one thing, in the years after King was killed, the movement of "runaway union shops" to the non-union South and West picked up considerably, and labor became much weaker. For King the labor movement up to the time of his death—especially the labor movement that he knew from the 1940s—was the one great exception to all the disappointments of American history. What he liked about the early labor movement in particular was its impatience: the total rejection of the idea that working people should be "patient" and "wait," the same things black Americans were being told. He saw the civil rights movement and the labor movement as linked or overlapping—he said so repeatedly.

And King was prescient: even before leaders of the AFL-CIO did, he worried about the future of the labor movement. Part of his genius was to realize as early as 1961 that *both* the unions and black Americans were in trouble thanks to the rise of a radical right that at the time most people still ignored. He told the AFL-CIO in 1961:

> And as we stand on the threshold of the twentieth century, a crisis confronts us both. Those who in the second half of the nineteenth century could not tolerate organized labor have had a rebirth of power and seek to regain the despotism of that era while retaining the wealth and privileges of the

twentieth century. Whether it be the ultra right wing in the form of Birch societies or the alliance which former President Eisenhower denounced, the alliance between big military and big business, or the coalition of southern Dixiecrats and northern reactionaries, whatever the form, these menaces now threaten everything decent and fair in American life. Their target is labor, liberals and the Negro people, not scattered "reds" or even Justice Warren, former Presidents Eisenhower and Truman and President Kennedy, who are in truth beyond the reach of their crude and vicious falsehoods.

He made clear in that 1961 speech that labor itself faced a crisis. In particular, he was already worrying about the decline of the industrial unions such as the UAW at a time when the organizing of service-sector workers had barely begun. That's why he called, well over fifty years ago, for a new kind of labor movement and for labor to reinvent itself.

Labor today faces a grave crisis, perhaps the most calamitous since it began its march from the shadows of want and insecurity. In the next ten to twenty years automation will grind jobs into dust as it grinds out unbelievable volumes of production. This period is made to order for those who would seek to drive labor into impotency by viciously attacking it at every point of weakness. . . . To find a great design to solve a grave problem labor will have to intervene in the political life of the nation to chart a course which distributes the abundance to all instead of concentrating it among a few.

King grasped that the civil rights movement would collapse if the labor movement collapsed. It is important to remember that the Civil Rights Act of 1964 depended on—or really assumed—the right of black Americans to organize: the ban on discrimination in Title VII of the Civil Rights Act was emphatically directed at unions not only because they were racist but also because movement leaders like King, A. Philip Randolph, and Bayard Rustin, all "labor men," understood that unions were crucial if black Americans were to have a better way of life. The tragedy is that at the very moment Title VII of the Civil Rights Act started to have a real effect on at least the industrial unions, those unions were already starting to collapse. That is exactly what worried King. He saw that the crisis the civil rights movement faced was that the labor movement did not know how to save itself. He became impatient with labor not just because it was slow to bring blacks into the trades (and it still is in many cases), but because it was slow to reinvent itself. As he said on another occasion, to the Illinois State AFL-CIO, "Labor cannot stand still or it will fall backward."

Furthermore, King got something else right: namely, that it was crucial to put civil rights laws in place as soon as possible, while there was still a large black population in the South, and thus permit black Americans to join enough whites to build a labor movement strong enough to check the right wing there. It is one of the tragedies of American history that so many blacks left the South before the civil rights laws took effect. In a sense, the civil rights laws came too late to stop this depopulation and preserve the chance for biracial majorities to vote for more unions in the South.

Martin Luther King, A. Philip Randolph, and Bayard Rustin— the three who organized the March on Washington to push for a minimum wage of $1.95 an hour—knew that the right to join a union was a civil right, just as a right to a minimum wage was a civil right. Does anyone doubt that King and the others would be in the Fight for 15 today? Their shades implore us: "The Civil Rights Act is our legacy—please extend it to the labor movement!"

Now let me give the perspective of a working labor lawyer to explain why the Civil Rights Act is so much better than our labor law. Consider the limitations of the existing law, the Wagner Act, which friends in bars or at parties sometimes nudge me to explain to the uninitiated: "Tell them what it's like." Well, it goes like this. Let's suppose an employer says, "I'm going to fire you in violation of the Wagner Act for exercising your right to organize. Now go see what you can do about it." In other words, he or she admits to a violation. At that point, the employee can only file an unfair labor practice charge, which is likely to be ignored unless the union has a lawyer draft it and spends money to get behind it. Then the employee has to prevail on the Office of the General Counsel at the NLRB, likely headed by an interim appointee, to file a complaint based upon the charge. That's already a lot of work and a fair amount of time. But wait, there's more: for the next one or two (or three) years, the employee has to prepare and then wait for a trial-type hearing before an administrative law judge. The speed may depend on how much Congress is willing to spend on the NLRB's budget that year. Then, after a weeklong hearing, there may or may not be success; if there is success, then there's the appeal to the full NLRB in D.C. This may take a total of two to three to four years. Then—even if there is a full NLRB complement in place that allows the NLRB to rule in the worker's favor, and even if the worker has miraculously continued to fight up until this point—even then, years later, the worker *still* cannot go back to work. The NLRB has to petition the U.S. Court of Appeals, which may not get around to the case for two more years. Finally, if you're lucky, there is a reinstatement order—several years after the illegal firing.

Now, let's say that rather than starve all this time, you got another job, one at the same damn $9 an hour. It's quite possible that if you found another job right away, the boss who fired you owes nothing in "lost" back pay. Nothing: not a cent, even if you "win." That's our modern labor law.

And if you're naive enough to go back to your old job, the boss can count to ten before firing you again.

Now suppose we were to have a labor civil rights act. Here's what you can then do if by putting on a union button you end up being fired.

First, you can dash to federal court in just a few minutes rather than wait for the NLRB to deal with it—maybe—in four or five years. Once in court, as a plain ordinary citizen, you as an Auto-Zone employee would have more legal remedies than the entire AFL-CIO could now obtain. Let me list just a few:

A temporary restraining order against your being demoted, so crucial to dispel any chilling effect on the union vote that is coming up

A preliminary injunction, based on likelihood of succeeding

A jury trial with a chance to get compensatory damages—not just for back pay but also for emotional distress, your hurt feelings

Punitive damages, so the jury can teach your employer a lesson

If all that sounds good, that's the least of it. You have two much bigger sticks. First, you can take discovery. You have the equivalent of subpoena power—except it's even better than a formal subpoena. You just send the boss a request for production of documents and say, in effect, "I want every written scrap of paper, including e-mails, about your attempt to bust the union."

After all, that's connected to your demotion to the back room.

Then you can pull in the store manager, the HR person, maybe the boss, and take depositions from everyone under oath—oh, not too long, but, say, just up to seven hours. They have to sit

there and think with every answer: "I'm under oath. Is this per-
jury?" Some say that modern discovery is the equivalent of wa-
terboarding. That's not fair, but it's true that it's anything but
pleasant.

Now you may scoff: "Come on, level with us—you aren't going
to win all these cases, right?"

Little children, it does not matter: the slugfest known as "civil"
discovery—a discovery of one's stamina, a brutal inquiry into the
operation of the company—will end up deciding more cases than
judges or juries do. Trust me: I do these cases.

Yet I do happen to think that, at least at first, employees may
"win" in the conventional sense of "win." Think back to the 1960s
and 1970s: plaintiff lawyers won lots of civil rights cases not because judges were so liberal (especially in the South) but because
the race-baiting was so overt. Bosses were hurling racial insults.
Today's union busting is just as overt and grotesque. It's hard to
see how we can lose: the purpose of firing a union activist is to
send a message. Union busting *has* to be overt, unlike the firing
of an employee for race or age or sex. Race and sex bias can go
underground. It can be in the subconscious. But if union busting is not overt, what's the point? Unless the message is loud
and clear, it does no good. That's the job of the union-busting
consultant: make sure the employees see it. Even if the jurors
personally do not care about unions, the judge instructs them
on the law. In my own experience and that of others, jurors take
those legal instructions pretty seriously. Of course, over time the
antiunion animus will go underground, but to the extent it goes
underground it stops working. We actually *want* things to get to
the point that the employer can "win." When we get to the point
where employers need to conceal their hostility to unions, we will
be living in a different, better world. In that sense, nothing would
be better for the labor movement than to start losing these cases.
Finally, even if the employer "wins," it still loses. A memo goes

out to the human resources department: "Make sure we never do this again."

Remember the Paula Jones case: a lawyer, not even a very good one, nearly brought down a sitting president. Any pro se litigant in this country has more power to take discovery than the entire AFL-CIO when it gets behind a worker in an NLRB case. I don't care who's on the U.S. Supreme Court or even whether labor ever wins a case. Just having that power to poke through the defendant's house has brought a lot of social change in this country.

My civil rights lawyer friends say, "It's not so easy to win a race discrimination case. I haven't won one in years." Yes, but do employers pay big dollars for a consultant to come in and tell them how to stomp on African Americans?

No.

Do employers fire African Americans to send a message about how much they just *hate* black people?

No.

They discriminate—but not like that.

But that's exactly what happens when an employer brings in a consultant to bust a union and demotes you to the back room for putting on that union button.

So I say to my civil rights lawyer friends, "In Title VII cases now, do you win the reprisal suits? Do you win suits after your client is fired just for filing a charge with the Equal Employment Opportunity Commission?"

"Sure, those are easy."

"Well, it's the same thing."

Then they smile: "Oh, I get it."

At any rate, that's the big stick: to have a lawyer able to rifle through the files at the company store, look at everything it's doing to stop the union. That in itself is a form of "worker control," if the worker finds a lawyer who smells a good case.

That brings us to another difference: the suits would come

from everywhere. It's no longer a matter of what kind of litigation the union could afford. The union has no money to defend you even at the pitiful hourly rates that we union lawyers get. That's why you have no right to organize. It costs money to have "rights." Labor under the Wagner Act has no money. All the dues money in the world is not enough to do a tenth of the organizing we need to do, and that's why unions are especially loath to organize in right-to-work states. If they win, and the employees still don't join the union and kick in dues, they never get a return on the money and effort. But the civil rights laws are self-funding, so you're not limited to a dwindling number of labor lawyers being paid at $175 an hour. You can go to a fancy lawyer, and he or she might recover a $350 or higher hourly rate, on par with other lawyers.

That's the second big stick, as big as the one for discovery. If you win, or even if you settle, you can get your legal fees covered. Then the employer, not the union, funds these cases. The employer, not the union, pays the "cost" of these rights.

That cost shifting is a sea change in management-labor relations. It's why these kinds of cases settle. It's not the possibility of damages but the mounting legal fees, charged at what may turn out to be $350 an hour. Let's say the case goes the distance. There is a settlement before trial. "You'd better not chance this." How much will it cost?

It is quite possible that this defendant, which may be just a retail store with fifty people, would have to cough up $200,000 just in your legal fees, its own legal fees, discovery and deposition costs, etc. My friends say, "Yes, tell me how this big change in the law is going to help us organize a little retail shop?" Well, *that's* how it will. Indeed, the civil rights law works far better for these little two-bit organizing drives than it does for the big change-the-world or let's-bring-down-Walmart organizing drives.

Remember, this conflict is "asymmetrical," as the lieutenant colonels like to say at West Point. The employee pushing the suit is paying nothing, while the employer is paying $350 (or $500) an hour every time its lawyer files a motion to extend time. The employer is bleeding cash just for one lowly demotion of a guy with a union button—a harm that would pass unnoticed now.

When I settle civil rights cases, the other side is only faintly interested in what the client may be owed. The question is, what am *I* owed? "What are your fees?" In a labor civil rights act, this "fee shifting" could be a more important safeguard of the right to organize than the existence of the right itself.

Forget "winning." The way modern litigation changes our culture does not depend on anyone's "winning." It is about imposing costs—not just financial but emotional—the costs of intrusion, the fear, quite justifiable fear, that my rights are going to be violated.

So why has organized labor not proposed this before?

Well, for organized labor, there is a catch. Extended to labor, the Civil Rights Act would mean that anyone—with or without old labor's permission—can go out and bring down an employer. The labor movement will be different if everyone has access to a lawyer. That means old labor will have to let go of its exclusive control of the labor law remedies. Everyone can go out and get a lawyer and take a shot at organizing. And these really will be the employee's and not the union's lawyers.

Note that it is also a way of whittling down the contempt that any manager might pour down on a lowly employee. Nothing creates more equality than a deposition, where your manager has to answer under oath the questions that you or your lawyer can frame with a certain premeditated malice.

At any rate, all this would change the division of labor between union and union member. Right now, under current law, members depend on union bureaucracies and union-paid lawyers to fight their battles; only the unions have the clout to get the attention of a federal agency like the NLRB with its scarce resources for enforcing the law. Only unions with compulsory dues can come up with the financial resources to see the case through (though just barely). But if labor law becomes just another civil rights law, those days are over.

But why not have the Employee Free Choice Act (EFCA), which labor was pushing in the last session of Congress? Isn't it better just to speed up elections and then—if there's trouble—have the NLRB come in and actually *write* the contract?

I'm all in favor of EFCA. Mandatory arbitration of first contracts—that's great. *Too* great: we are just not going to get it. It's hard to imagine that Congress would pass such a law—have the NLRB write the labor contracts? Come on. Yes, I'm in favor of it! But let's suppose a miracle happens and we *do* get it: remember the uproar in Washington, D.C., over the NLRB's challenge to Boeing for moving the Dreamliner to South Carolina? Imagine how Congress would erupt over an NLRB that slapped a whole labor contract on Caterpillar! Above all, we cannot channel an entire labor movement through the bottleneck of a single agency in Washington, D.C., with Congress throwing fits. What movement would want to be choked off in that way?

The great thing about the civil rights approach is that Congress turns over the enforcement of the law to working people themselves. It privatizes the enforcement of labor law. From that point on, no one in Washington, D.C., knows what's going on. There are no novel constitutional problems. Courts see thousands of these cases under this or that civil rights law: age, handicap, gender, pension, etc. It is a legal remedy that at least in a constitutional sense is good to go. And the workers possess a power that they have never had before, beyond even the dreams of the New Dealers: the power to take testimony and subpoena documents. Every working American would have the same—or, really, greater power—than a federal agency. And no member of Congress or editorial writer at the *Wall Street Journal* will object, or even hear about the suit, because this is all private litigation, without any Obama-type involvement, and there is nothing more American than our right to pull each other into court.

Yes, many will still scoff: "I doubt this will win over the country."

"Yes, but at least people will understand it."

You can go into a bar and try to explain EFCA for half an hour to each patron, and at the end they'll just be staring glassy-eyed into their beer mugs. But making unionizing a civil right? That takes all of fifteen seconds to explain.

What American can object to a private individual's right to file a lawsuit? It is often said that labor, with its whiff of collectivity, is not part of American culture. Well, this proposal makes it fit right in. The French have strikes; we have lawsuits. It all fits perfectly into the American way of life.

And if I'm wrong and it does not fit in, it soon will. "We can't use laws to change the culture." Sure we can. Indeed, culture *is* the law—as any good anthropologist would say—and nowhere is that more true than in the United States.

Perhaps some union lawyers will say, "But your proposal only deals with firings. That's not enough. Our real problem is 'captive' meetings." The boss, yelling, with veins popping—people leave, trembling, after an hour, terrified for their jobs. It's worse to bring them in one by one. Yes, captive meetings are scary—but if captive meetings are a problem, it's because the employers can fire anyone at any time. They take place in the context of the boss picking off two or three ringleaders. That's what the Civil Rights Act would stop. The very existence of a captive meeting would help prove the "antiunion animus" needed to win the case—now it is just one more damn thing for which the employer can be deposed. The boss has to worry about the captive meeting as much as the employee. Now people can talk back. The employees who support the drive no longer have to whisper in the dark. They can update their status on Facebook. They can announce themselves and come out into the open. And it would be a profoundly serious risk for an employer to fire or even demote such an employee.

Let's get to the final concern of the union-side lawyer: "Our problem is getting a first contract at all." But in my version, by signing the "first" contract, or any contract, the employer is out of legal liability. It's easy to draft such a provision in the law— once the employer signs a collective bargaining agreement with the union, any claim under a labor civil rights act would have to go to contract arbitration. In arbitration, there are no depositions, there are no legal fees.

And the employer's old incentive for *not* signing a first contract—to go on and bust the union—is the kind of overreach that may land the employer back in court. Do you really want to go back and have your deposition taken again?

At any rate, there is no alternative—Congress will never pass a law to let the government write contracts for Caterpillar, Bain Capital, or anyone else. And even if it did, the federal government would now have a power that even labor might come to dread.

I wouldn't want the GOP to impose a contract on *me*.

But let's not worry—it won't happen. Indeed, the question is: how do we get even a civil rights law in place?

## 2. Get Rid of the Filibuster—or Think About a Deal

We can't have a labor movement without the power to disrupt. That was true in the 1930s. It's true for any social movement. Yes, we need more strikes. But to bring back a labor movement, we need other ways to disrupt. As argued here, we also need litigation to disrupt what employers do. If we put in a labor civil rights act, we can give this power to disrupt to individuals who can go into federal court with their own lawyers—and recover legal fees if they win. This would also break organized labor's stifling control over the right to organize. That's crucial: as in the 1930s, we need a legal framework that lets people organize without the labor hierarchy necessarily knowing or consenting to everything they're doing.

But how do we get this through Congress?

Well, we can always say that this civil rights–type litigation is now as American as, oh, the right to own a gun. But it's really a matter of getting the votes, enough votes to beat a Senate filibuster.

Of course at the moment a gerrymandered House is in the grip of the GOP. And thanks to such gerrymandering isn't the House lost to our side, at least until after 2020, when the next redistricting occurs? And even after 2020, the Democrats may not take back enough GOP-gerrymandered state legislatures to redraw the maps. So what hope then? But there is always the Supreme Court, the only department of government capable of ending gridlock like this. Suppose that the Democrats can hold the White House up to 2020 and put in just a single liberal justice to replace one of the conservative five. The change to our "unwritten constitution" could be colossal. One day, in particular, there may be not a five-to-four majority to uphold GOP gerrymandering as in cases like *LULAC v. Perry* (2004) but a five-to-four majority to *end* it. Still, would that be enough to flip the House? According to number-crunching geographers, even *neutral* redistricting favors the GOP. Democrats, alas, tend to hole up in cities rather than spread out evenly throughout the states.

I wish we could get more Democratic voters to move.

Still, there are three reasons to bet against the GOP. First, even neutral redistricting would loosen the Tea Party's grip on the House; at least that chamber would be more in play. Second, the nonwhite population, which favors Democrats, *is* spreading out into those nooks and crannies of our states. Indeed, the balance might already have swung against the GOP if the right-to-work laws hadn't given labor such a perverse incentive not to organize in so many places. As a result, there is now no infrastructure in place in some states to take advantage of the demographic changes that are now occurring; in states like Kansas, the Tea Party has had the place to itself for too long, with no real check on its bullying of its opponents on the left or even its own supporters. Indeed, by acting "rationally" and acting on the "incentive" not to organize, labor helps contribute to the rise of a much too radical right. Yet this may be about to change, even in Kansas, where the nonwhite population is growing and both nonlabor and labor organizing are growing.

Third and finally—and let me just dream here—the GOP may destroy itself. Well, I'm free to wish for it.

Meanwhile, the Senate or the filibuster is still the deadly serious block to labor law reform. After all, sooner or later the House is probably going to flip, but the filibuster may never go away. While its ability to block presidential nominees was cut back in November 2013, it is still able to block any new laws. Of course, it is a huge gain that GOP filibusters will no longer block nominees to the NLRB. Now at least the NLRB can function.

The filibuster rule really is the ultimate "labor law" in this country. Even in the late 1970s, an early use of the modern "silent" or "procedural" filibuster was to block Democratic nominees to the NLRB. The filibuster—originally in place to protect slavery, which means its use actually helped precipitate the Civil War and then protect Jim Crow for nearly a century thereafter—has always existed in part to ensure a pool of either slave or low-wage labor. And that's still its role. Twice in my adult lifetime, a Senate filibuster has blocked labor law reform that the House had passed. And let's cut the nonsense of there being sixty Democrats in the Senate to make everything OK—sixty is not enough. Somebody's vote is always going to be for sale.

The hope is that new and younger senators—especially Tom

Udall of New Mexico and Jeff Merkley of Oregon—keep pressing to get rid of the rule altogether. I think the fate of this country is in many ways up to the two of them. But let's suppose they fail, and the filibuster stays in place.

Then what?

Then we have to offer something the right wants so badly that it will let through a civil rights act for labor.

Well, let's consider what the right wants. There's not much labor could give up, because it's already lost everything. Do they want a ban on strikes? No one strikes anyway. There's no chip we can give up—there's nothing to negotiate away.

Oh, but wait—there is one thing. Think about right-to-work laws not only in Michigan but in Wisconsin, Ohio, and other states: the right would love to get a *national* right-to-work law. They want that so badly because they are so convinced it will keep labor from pouring money into races that there just might be a deal.

I'm a labor lawyer. Right now, under the existing structure, I would fight to the death to stop a national right-to-work law. So long as we can't organize, we need all the dues we can get. We're in a crisis. And I grasp fully the unfairness of the free riders. Why let them off the hook?

No, it's wrong, wrong, wrong. Besides, we in labor need that dues money more than ever to defend Social Security and Medicare.

On the other hand . . . what if we got the Labor Civil Rights Act?

As Carlyle said of the Reform Act of 1867, it would be like "shooting Niagara." While a national right-to-work law might diminish labor's cash and clout, the Civil Rights Act might make labor bigger. It could end up with more money, though it might have to scramble to sell itself to members.

At least I'm willing to consider this possibility—just consider it. What makes labor such an alien thing is that it can take a chunk of people's paychecks without their consent. In collectivist Europe, it's too much to ask, and nothing like it exists. In "socialist" Europe, even the "fair share" or the reduction in the full dues payment that we allow to those who "opt out" of union membership here would not be regarded as fair. Why would a European who does not want to be in a union have to pay anything? And if they feel that way in semi-socialist Europe—well, let's seriously consider how people must feel in red-blooded Tennessee. In the free-market United States, it's hard to imagine now how such a compulsory payment ever came to be.

But in these other countries, like Germany, aren't there free riders? Yes, there are free riders. Workers may be more politically sophisticated in Germany, or the Philippines, or Nigeria, or wherever, but there are free riders in just about every country in the world. On the other hand, as pointed out above, it's much easier to organize in these countries, so there are far more potential members who can kick in and compensate for free riders. And some people will pay voluntarily. It's true in Germany. It's true in our own right-to-work states. After all, some of the 11.3 percent who make up the unionized share of America's workforce do live in right-to-work states, and even in free-rider America some people have the decency to pay voluntarily.

And if we had right-to-work laws not just in twenty-four states but everywhere, it would take away a lot of the populist appeal for shackling labor. The argument for labor law reform would then be: "Hey, now, it isn't such a big deal to have a union in place. It's not like anyone *has* to pay."

Still, there are powerful arguments not to give it up. Look, I would propose this only as part of a deal, and I understand the argument that no deal might be good enough to warrant it. *Never, never, never*—and those who say "Never" may turn out to be right. But let's face it: we may not have the ability to hang on to the current system, because of either Supreme Court action or the creep of right-to-work laws into more and more states. Besides, let's take a deep breath and think how the current system looks to many Americans. Making it easier to organize really is a bigger deal if it means thousands of people who voted against the union now have to pay their "fair share" every week out of their meager paychecks whether they really want to do it or not. As long as that system is in place, our side has to realize: labor law reform will be a harder sell with *some* people than it should be, as long as it comes with agency shop. It's going to be a harder sell with people who might object if there is no "exit" from the union or "voice" over how the union is run.

And as long as it comes with agency shop, it's going to be much harder to get a right to join a union. That's just a fact.

But isn't it harder to organize in a right-to-work state? I have no doubt it's harder to organize in right-to-work states! Employers are nastier in those states. But it's also harder because there is so small a labor presence. In turn, that's at least in part because labor is less likely to "invest" in organizing in states where the new members can opt out of paying dues.

As a result, there isn't much of a union "culture" in those states. And the tinier the union culture, the more alien and intrusive a union seems. The very fact that unions can't force people in the South into paying dues should make it easier to organize, but unions forfeit even that advantage by the way they denounce as an act of oppression a liberty that should actually work in their favor.

Of course it would be unsettling—even terrifying—if labor entered a grand bargain that created a real right to organize but gave up the union shop. For one thing, in a very short time, labor here would have to transform itself and become more like labor in Europe. It would have to scramble. It would have to sell itself every day to the membership. It would always have to put on a "show."

Maybe it rakes your leaves. Maybe it starts delivering pizza. As a member, I might favor compulsory dues: "I don't want freeloaders." I might be horrified to see my union's clout drop even for a brief period. But I might also like to live in a world where labor had to sell itself—where its survival depended, as in Europe, on its ability to cater to me.

To all my friends who faint dead away when I suggest this only as a quid pro quo for the right to organize—*no, never!*—I ask only this question: what is the one union town left in America? Answer: Las Vegas. That's where UNITE HERE has organized the maids. That's why old labor still has its conventions out there. But Nevada is a right-to-work state. It's hard to get figures even from UNITE HERE, and they may be out of date by the time this book is published, but maybe 70 percent or so of the UNITE HERE members in Las Vegas voluntarily pay dues.

Or consider the National Treasury Employees Union (NTEU). It should not even exist. First, it is organizing IRS agents, who have to be the least promising union material in America. Second, it has nothing to offer, or so it would seem. The NTEU can't strike, of course. Federal law prohibits it. The NTEU can't even bargain wages! Congress does that. Yet over 70 percent of IRS agents and other Treasury employees voluntarily pay dues. The NTEU is scrambling for its money every day, coming up with some service or other. I know a lawyer there who is also a business agent and who regularly gets behind a grill and barbecues for the members who show up at meetings. In short, they hustle, and people respond. It's the leadership and not the rank and file who bow and scrape.

If you think labor is in good shape at 11, or 10, or 9 percent of the workforce, then none of this will make any sense to you. It will be absolutely unacceptable. "I'd rather labor die first!"

What's worse: to represent four million workers, with everyone paying dues, or to represent twenty million, with one in five paying dues? Personally, I'd go with the twenty million, even if the dues from the checkoff came out exactly the same.

To be sure, it's not a choice labor faces *now* but it might be one day, in a different Congress, with a Democratic House. And while it is not pleasant, we ought at least to consider the possibility. If it came down to the difference between having a new type of labor movement in the European fashion and nothing at all, shouldn't it at least be discussed?

## 3. Think Corporate—Not Labor—Law

This means bringing back a form of "labor control" that does not involve the labor movement as such. Now it seems impossible that in the United States working people could ever elect even a single director to a corporate board. "Not in my lifetime." But the next lifetime may not be so far off. A stakeholder model—the full-strength German one or the weaker imitations elsewhere in Europe—might fill the gap where no stockholder model exists. The publicly traded corporation is losing its appeal: many of these companies have gone "private," and without any public shareholders there is no one, nothing, to stop the place from being looted. After all, under U.S. corporate law, there is a fiduciary duty not to the stockholders but *to the company*. In the not-for-profit sector, things are arguably worse: there are no shareholders at all. The boards of these "charities"—some of our biggest companies, with staggering assets—perpetuate themselves with no accountability at all. One board elects the next board. And in that respect, are the not-for-profits *really* any different from the publicly traded for-profit companies? The problem with the publicly traded companies—a problem that Dodd-Frank only weakly addressed—is that even the stockholders cannot put in place "outside" directors, except on rare occasions. That's why there is a bonus culture, since these corporate boards have no outside directors at all and there is not even a labor movement as a check.

So our corporate model has broken down. Otherwise, CEOs would not make up to $25 million a year. Whatever the merits of the old classical model of stockholder control, it simply no longer exists. There is no federal chartering of corporations—and not much hope for it. And it would seem that no state can enact a different corporate model, since the corporations will just find a charter in another state. So what to do?

I can think of two things.

First, states do have more control over not-for-profit corporations, which are relatively more captive. It is harder for them to escape from, oh, socialist Vermont. A state could insist that nurses and kitchen help and all the other employees of a hospital have the right to elect half of the directors of the corporate board. And even with for-profit firms, the state could exempt from state income tax any company that let its workers elect a third or half of the members of the board. States already compete with each other to throw millions of dollars in tax breaks at companies; it seems no big deal to toss in just one more. In New Jersey, there is already such a proposal, the Garden State Manufacturing Jobs Act.

Will everyone try it? Of course not—but it's enough if one or two start-ups show that it is possible. It plants the idea of European co-determination on North American soil. Nor would it be "preempted" by federal labor law and deemed a state law interference with collective bargaining. I want to stress that point. A specific state law that allowed nurses to elect one of their colleagues to a board would not have anything to do with collective bargaining. After all, that elected nurse is not there as a director to discuss wages and benefits or to take part in collective bargaining at all. Yes, it may be just one state law at first. But think how the Massachusetts health care law turned into a model for Obama's national health care years later. Maybe New Jersey will lead the way.

Here's another example: a change of law in just *one* of the fifty states could let employees sue CEOs and directors for breach of fiduciary duty *to the corporation*. Such a law would have allowed laid-off employees to sue Mitt Romney and his friends at Bain when they sucked the capital out of solvent companies and forced them into bankruptcy. It's true that by not incorporating in the state, a corporation might avoid the law. But some big corporations—like not-for-profit hospitals—would not be able to escape so easily. And such laws will inevitably catch some for-profit corporations and at least create a model for possible federal legislation.

But up to now, we have just discussed changes affecting the corporate boards, the role of the CEOs and directors. What about a works council, at a plant level?

Yes, even that can happen here, at least at the state level. Let's say that a state wanted to stop wage theft but lacked agency resources. It would be perfectly legal for a state to require a company like Walmart to have a worker committee—say, to monitor whether Walmart is paying what might be a state minimum wage higher than the federal minimum or complying with state laws. I borrow this idea from the great Clyde W. Summers, a long-time professor of law at the University of Pennsylvania. In his view, state law could authorize the workers to elect that committee. Other state laws, such as state health and safety laws, could require additional committees. These monitoring committees, elected by workers, may be a long way from a German-type works council. But at least it plants the idea of worker control in our North American soil.

I know some readers will think: "Oh come on—the states?" It seems so retro to say they can still be the "laboratories of democracy." But the Progressives, Louis Brandeis and others, used to think so in their time. Some states were the first to try out the laws that became the program of the New Deal. Let's think of ourselves as being like the Progressives in 1912. Twenty years to the next New Deal is not *so* far away.

Finally, there is hope for federal intervention, even now— specifically, the presidential power over government contracts, discussed in chapter 5. Once more, a Democratic president can try to use the procurement authority to help introduce a bit of corporate democracy into this country. Specifically, an executive order could state that *other things being equal* the federal government will give some favorable consideration in procurement decisions to those corporate vendors whose boards are partly elected by their employees. Under Clinton, as noted earlier, a much cruder use of the procurement power to punish companies that violated federal labor law failed to make it through the very conservative U.S. Court of Appeals for the District of Columbia, where federal regulations go to die. But thanks to the reform of the filibuster over nominees to that court, it should be a much friendlier forum going forward.

By all means, let's keep pressing the Democrats, since that's what King would do.

But what if all of this comes to naught?

# 11

# If All Else Fails

Of course no civil rights law may ever pass. Democrats may give up on labor. Congress may be dysfunctional forever. Even so, there are at least two other ways the labor movement could reinvent itself.

## Part One: Globalization Will Save Us

If all else fails, maybe globalization will save us. Wait, isn't globalization what wrecked labor in the first place? For the United States, that's always seemed dubious: after all, thanks in part to globalization, our GDP per capita keeps going up. So logically, for the same reason, median income per capita should have been going up as well: why then put the blame on globalization for wages being stagnant?

But even if one were to assume globalization did wreck labor, it may now paradoxically be the one thing that can save it. The premise here is Harvard labor economist Richard Freeman's point. Compared to the United States, the workplace in other high-income countries is more egalitarian: at least there still are unions or some form of worker representation.

As a result, if globalization increases, so does the possibility that foreign companies may try out a more egalitarian workplace here.

Why would they do so? Like in a Joseph Conrad tale, they might just paddle on upriver to their colonial trading posts and lord it over us the same way our American managers do. And that might be all that ever happens. When Germans, Swedes, Belgians, and Japanese come here, they already treat American workers as disposable in a way they would never do back home. A friend of mine, a onetime labor attaché at the Germany embassy in Washington, D.C., used to complain that German managers would come over here and behave just as the American ones do. "I used to ask them," he said, 'Isn't our co-determination a good thing?' And in private they would agree with me. 'Yes, of course,' they would say, 'it is better to share power.' And so then I would ask, 'Then why not do it here in America?' They didn't have an answer."

"So," I said, "what's your answer?"

"I think . . . whenever people are free to take power, they just will—they can't help themselves."

On the other hand, the logic of globalization would seem to call for a uniform approach, at least within a single firm's global operations. That's the hope for us "one-world" types. While there may never be global labor regulation at a state or governmental level, we might have something like it within particular private firms. A works council in the home country may evolve into a global works council.

So if a European firm one day were to plant just a sprig of worker democracy in the soil of the New World, then it might begin to spread—yes, it could replicate here, on our own continent. After all, there are precedents for such things that go back to Cortés.

But some company has to start the planting. So far every firm has balked. Look at the German auto plants of Volkswagen, BMW, and Daimler in the South. It is sometimes said that such German companies have an interest in "exporting" the German model. While the point can be overstated, it's not completely wrong. A company like Volkswagen not only has a works council at its principal base in Wolfsburg, Germany, it now also has a global works council, with members from works councils at its other plants all over the world: Poland, Russia, the Czech Republic, and elsewhere. The members of the global works council, if not Volkswagen management, do have an interest in spreading the model: not just to Poland next door but to Mexico, India, China, and yes—even to Chattanooga, Tennessee.

It's true that in February 2014 the United Auto Workers lost the election to organize Volkswagen's Chattanooga plant. So it seems unlikely for a long time, right?

Maybe—but despite the defeat at Volkswagen, there is still reason to think that globalization may save us. For one thing, though defeated, the UAW has not given up yet. The UAW has just created a new local and claims Volkswagen will recognize the local without an election if it signs up enough workers. Volkswagen is not commenting but has not rejected the claim either.

An even if *that* fails, the UAW could still just go and demand to bargain—just for those willing to be UAW members and no one else. Of course that would be a big break in the UAW way of doing things. Having gone "European" in seeking a works council, the UAW might just as well start bargaining the way they do in Europe too—that is, without a majority, without being the "exclusive representative" of everyone, and just for those who pay dues to be members. The UAW lost only by a vote of 715 to 626; well, it could plausibly start bargaining for that goodly number. At least in Europe, that would constitute enough support to start bargaining. Say to Volkswagen, "Let's do it here the way you do it over there."

I know: people say the UAW isn't ready to do this kind of thing. Most unions aren't—not yet. But that's exactly what is happening with Fight for 15. It's the logic of survival: labor in the private sector is shrinking. The weaker we become, the harder it is to win a majority. OK. Let's just sign up and bargain for those who want to join.

The question is: in an age of globalization, to what extent is labor in America willing to act like other labor movements around the world?

That's why I think it is important to look back over the history of this organizing drive. Yes, the UAW lost. But that campaign marked some new approaches that give a bit of hope for the future. Let's begin with the biggest: for the first time, IG Metall, Germany's biggest union, lent significant support to an organizing drive in the United States. The Volkswagen works council also took on a major role. In the past, it has been rare for the workers of the world to pitch in for each other. It was a breakthrough that the UAW even *asked for help*. It is even more remarkable that Bob King, the UAW president, not only went to Germany and met with people at IG Metall but actually listened to them and took some of their advice.

King also sought help from Volkswagen management—he made extraordinary attempts not to be confrontational. Early on he went to management and said, "We want to organize, but we want to do this with you cooperatively—or not at all." From the beginning, King took the approach that he was going to do this only by consensus. Not once, by the way, has the UAW openly criticized the company.

So what's all this advice he took?

It was to offer Volkswagen a deal: where the UAW would

normally be the exclusive representative of every worker under Section 9(a) of the Wagner Act, it would now agree to a works council that the UAW would not control. It would give up its exclusive right to bargain "in-plant" issues: scheduling, use of temporaries, even discharges. In effect it was to tell Volkswagen, "Even though it's not our way, we'll do it the way you do in Germany."

Even coming in peace and not war, King faced resistance. For years Volkswagen had blamed the UAW for the failure of a U.S. plant in Pennsylvania, where a rash of wildcat strikes occurred. Actually, some say that the UAW had been very responsible and had tried to stop the strikes. The plant in the 1970s had failed because the particular model it was producing failed to sell. At any rate, King broke the resistance. He began meeting with Horst Neumann, the Volkswagen vice president for human relations. Soon they had a tentative agreement: if the UAW won the vote, it would consent to a German-type works council, elected by *all* the employees—blue collar, white collar, even middle managers. That's what mesmerized the business press: if the UAW won, a German-type works council would be coming to America. And who would think that such an advanced model of worker power— if not worker control—would be starting in the heart of Dixie?

Of course, as stated above, the UAW would pay a price: by agreeing to a works council, it would give up, partially, its right to be the "exclusive representative" of the workers. That's the right conferred by Section 9(a) of the Wagner Act. It would cede that right on all "noneconomic" issues, which made up many of the important issues in Chattanooga. It would retain that right only for wages, pensions, and health care.

Furthermore, on this works council, every employee would be eligible to serve. Keep in mind: people who hated the UAW could run. No U.S. labor union I know of has ever proposed so much *worker* control while giving up so much *union* control.

But there was no recognition of the union. Volkswagen still insisted on a majority vote. To be sure, it would be neutral. With a powerful works council and with its own employees making up half of the directors of the board, there is no way that Volkswagen could openly oppose a union.

But why not just recognize the UAW voluntarily?

Part of the reason is that there are different factions within Volkswagen management. Some were happy or happy enough to see the UAW lose. But surely a part of the reason was Volkswagen's fear of reprisal from Republicans in Tennessee.

Better to be like Pilate, shrug, and let the GOP and the UAW fight it out.

Before the vote, I even went to Germany to find out more about the deal. OK, I don't want to exaggerate. I had already had a plan to take a vacation in Berlin. Once the edgiest city in Europe, it is now one of the cushiest for lawyer types like me. I had a great time idling away every day at a local café, Cafemamas, a Latin American–style coffeehouse run by a woman from Istanbul. But I would sometimes think about Chattanooga and the upcoming vote that might change the world. Finally I did rouse myself to go to another coffeehouse, Café Einstein, and meet with a professor, Michael Fichter. He is an emeritus professor in labor relations at the Freie Universität and had been advising the UAW in connection with the vote.

I asked him about the trade-off: a contract with the UAW on wages and benefits in return for a German-type works council the UAW would not control.

"It's a brilliant idea in a right-to-work state," he said. "It gets rid of exclusive representation, except in some important areas. So the UAW can come in and say, 'Look, you aren't giving up all your rights to a union.'"

This might help de-demonize the UAW. It undercuts the line of every union buster: "Keep this Detroit-based institution from taking over!" If the works council is open to everyone, aren't the workers taking over instead?

It's also brilliant in another way: it's impossible to put in this model without the UAW. Before the UAW can give up (partially) being the exclusive representative, it first has to *be* the exclusive representative, certified as such under Section 9(a) of the Wagner Act. Otherwise, without the UAW to bless it, a works council *without a union* is almost certainly illegal under U.S. labor law. Technically, it would be no different from the old-fashioned "company union" that the Wagner Act had been passed in 1935 to ban. For Volkswagen to put in place the German model, it needs the UAW. And for the UAW to sign off, it has to be the exclusive representative of every worker in the plant.

Brilliant—but it's also risky.

"Yes," Michael said, "for the UAW it has an element of uncertainty. UAW members may not be a majority on the works council." Suppose the UAW wins the election by 55 to 45 percent. Then suppose the losing 45 percent of the hourly workers *and* the white-collar employees vote in an "anti-UAW" slate. The whole thing would go awry.

Still, as Michael pointed out, any union in a right-to-work state faces risks. People can drop out of the union at any time. They can stop paying dues. One day, in a right-to-work state, a union can turn around and find out it is not really representing anybody.

By this point in the fall of 2013, things already looked bad for the UAW. I spoke to one of the staff of the works council at Wolfsburg, Germany, and he was annoyed that Volkswagen would not voluntarily recognize the UAW without an election. The UAW, to be sure, had the majority of workers sign cards. I tried to explain why Volkswagen was insisting on an election. But still, to some on the works council, it was galling. Volkswagen had adopted a Global Labor Charter, a kind of bill of rights for all Volkswagen employees. Of all these rights, the paramount one is the right to join a union. It really was proposing to "export" its model, at least in language that to me as a lawyer looked contractual.

Remember, though, it's not a matter of Volkswagen agreeing to bargain: it was one of recognizing the UAW as the exclusive representative under Section 9(a) of the Wagner Act. That's no ordinary thing. In Germany, there is no such thing as IG Metall being the exclusive representative for every worker, whether that worker consents or not. The bargaining is limited to being on behalf of those who join the union. So Volkswagen could plausibly say: "Well, wait—this is different." It's a big step for Volkswagen to take voluntarily.

In short, when it comes to voluntary recognition, Volkswagen didn't have the nerve, at least back in February 2014. So a secret ballot election took place that month—and it turned out a bare majority of workers also didn't have the nerve.

It may have been the oddest single organizing drive of the new millennium. Normally, it's the employer that screams at the workers. Volkswagen didn't say a word. Instead, the Tea Party and the GOP establishment took up the job of screaming. Superficially, it was a puzzle. If Volkswagen didn't care, why did all these outsiders care? Well, that vote in Chattanooga could have changed the world. It would have been the fatal plant in the soil of the New World. It would have been the end of Dixie as we know it, if a de-demonized UAW were to show up down there. So it seemed the entire right converged on Chattanooga, and all its furies seemed to descend and fasten upon these poor Volkswagen workers, in the months leading up to the vote, with a rage that would have put the rage of Achilles in the shade. They included the National Right to Work Legal Defense Foundation, the Koch brothers (in the guise of the Competitive Enterprise

Institute), plus a brand-new entity called Southern Momentum, connected to Grover Norquist and probably funded by the Koch brothers too.

But even that was not enough: this was not just a crackpot Tea Party thing. The Republican Party establishment led the charge. The cry went up: "The South will be lost!" If even one plant organized in Tennessee, businesses would stop coming from the North. It would be a disaster for the whole state. The state's governor, Bill Haslam, predicted that if the UAW were to win, the state would be through. It now turns out he threatened to withhold over $300 million in tax credits that would normally have gone to Volkswagen for expansion of the plant if the UAW won. To be sure, Haslam's talk did not shake every worker. I spoke to one who said, "I'm as conservative as they come, but I think the governor has been a horse's ass."

Seriously, was he going to kick Volkswagen out of the state? As it turns out, it's pretty close to what Haslam and various state senators proposed to do. It wasn't a secret. State senator Bo Watson said that if the UAW won, it would be "exponentially more challenging" to get the credits.

The real leader of the fight, though, was Senator Bob Corker. The former mayor of Chattanooga, he believed he'd brought Volkswagen into the state, and now he felt betrayed. One works council staffer in Germany told me, "I'm convinced that somewhere in a drawer at Volkswagen, there's an agreement with Corker that there would never be a union." At any rate, Corker seemed furious. *Automotive News* quoted him saying the damage from a UAW victory in the South would last "for generations to come." All the dominoes would fall. "Then it's BMW," Corker said. "Then it's Mercedes, then it's Nissan, hurting the entire Southeast if they get momentum."

To some who doubt whether a single UAW victory would have

been so big a deal, Corker would put it up there with the burning of Atlanta.

Some were saying that the UAW would never press for an election. I thought so. But at least to my surprise, the UAW went ahead. By February the union seemed to think it was on top of things and could win the vote. It did seem that things had changed. The right was acknowledging a real prospect of defeat. Then, on February 19—the day of the vote—Senator Corker made a statement that had to give many workers pause. He said, "I've had conversations today and based on those am assured that should the workers vote against the UAW, Volkswagen will announce in the coming weeks that it will manufacture its new midsize SUV here in Chattanooga."

It was a shocking statement. Volkswagen management in Chattanooga denied it. But Corker replied that he had talked to the real decision makers in Germany—and of course he would never make this up.

It may have turned just enough workers against the UAW to lose the election. Even so, I find it all discouraging. I know Corker's statement was unnerving. But think of the power these workers could have had. A member of a works council could ask for virtually any company record. He or she could decide starting times and the use of temporary workers (if at all), and could override local managers in some cases.

And then there was the chance to be on the global works council, with other workers at Volkswagen plants around the world. It's depressing that people in this country would give up that power. When I was in Germany in the fall I had said bitterly to a German friend, "I'm afraid they'll hang back, as if it is too great a responsibility."

"Perhaps they should hang back," he said. "It is a great responsibility."

Yes, maybe Americans aren't up for it. But that can't be right. Thanks to a UAW press officer, I did talk on the phone to two of the pro-union workers down there. These two were up for it. Discussing the UAW's whole new approach, one of them was saying, "That's what is so exciting about this. It's not going to be 'us' versus 'them.' It's all of us working together."

He had even visited Germany to meet with some on the global works council. He said, "They're involved in things like—product placement." He paused. "We'll never be where we should be unless we're part of it."

Of course American workers should be part of those decisions. After all, the German model, a rival model, is here to stay. We may have turned down works councils in the United States for now, but the UAW is likely to try again. The Chattanooga plant may indeed expand, and the UAW has indicated it might seek a new election at that time. Works councils will certainly go on existing in Germany in the meantime. In Germany a reporter told me, "There used to be a debate about them here. But the debate is now over." He said that during the financial crisis of 2009, the works councils proved how valuable they were. When the Germans introduced the Kurzarbeit, a system of keeping workers on part-time with supplemental pay from the government, the works councils made the staffing decisions that prevented thousands of layoffs.

Members of the global works council come from Mexico, Argentina, and India to take part in major decisions. What happens when Volkswagen workers in China organize to demand works councils and when China joins the global works council, while workers in America are completely shut out?

It can't last. Yes, I know: what Corker and Watson and Haslam did will be a message to all southern politicians. Go ahead, make any threat you like. The National Labor Relations Board will do nothing—it's too afraid of Congress. Be like Nikki Haley, governor of South Carolina, who says she will use her high heels to stomp on any union that comes into the state. I know our side has to get these politicians to back off. But it may be a good sign, in a way, that the government, the governor, state legislators, a U.S. senator have now had to step out and do the screaming and let voters see exactly what is going on. The "new" South is starting to look like a decrepit, backward thing, out of step with the global economy, and worried about the crack-up of the entire region if even a single union wins. The awkward intervention of Corker—and all the money poured in by the right—may be a sign not of their growing strength but of a coming political collapse.

Perhaps it is true Volkswagen is now ready to voluntarily recognize the UAW if a majority sign authorization cards.

But maybe none of this will happen.

Maybe globalization will not save us. But there may be yet another way for a labor movement to come back.

## Part Two: Give Up Exclusive Representation

Yes, if all else fails, do exactly what the right wants. Give up "exclusive representation." Let me be plain: I mean more than just giving in on right-to-work laws, which I admit I would still hate to do. I mean more than letting people opt out of paying dues. Rather, if things get really bad, stop trying to represent "everyone." Stop doing "secret ballot" elections for that purpose. Stop the "majority vote" thing. Stop trying to get "certifications" to be the exclusive representative under Section 9(a) of the Wagner Act. Just represent *only* the people—be it 40 percent, or 30, or fewer—who sign up, take the oath, and pay the dues, and forget everyone else.

Why not do that?

Forget the elections, forget the card check, forget the whole clunky NLRB machinery that grinds out these certificates of exclusive representation, the thing that enrages the far right.

Since we may have no choice anyway, why not do what they do in Europe and most other countries and just represent the people who want to join?

In the United States, we say, often in a scoffing way, these countries have "nonmajority" bargaining or even "minority" bargaining.

I made the mistake of using that term with a German friend. He practically exploded: "Don't call it 'minority bargaining'! Call it 'members-only' bargaining!"

OK, let's call it members-only bargaining.

Like other European labor types, he was exasperated with the way we insist on *either* representing everyone in a bargaining unit *or* just walking away. To Germans it's no surprise that the plant in Chattanooga should be hard to organize.

"If we had to get 51 percent of the vote in Germany," my friend said, "we wouldn't have anyone in the unions either." That's the advantage of members-only bargaining. It recognizes that most people aren't heroes.

But since some people are, let's represent them. And as one example, let's go back to Chattanooga. I bet the plant has plenty of workers who would make a world-class "rank and file," men and women who dream about being in the UAW, though none may be paying dues right now. After all, 626 workers did vote to join. Generally, I believe there are far, far more working-class heroes than pundits of this country realize. How do I know? I have seen plenty of them. I am sure other union-side lawyers, organizers, business agents, research staff, and elected officers would all say the same thing: "I've seen them with my own eyes." I know there are enough of these people to inspire the rest of us to keep slogging away, even as labor seems to go into a deeper decline. So why not represent them? As far as anyone really knows, in terms of the raw number of working Americans ready to strike if only they could, our labor movement may be the strongest it has ever been.

But all those people—we don't bother to represent them, because they may be just 40 percent instead of 50 percent *plus* one inside a plant. We in labor refuse to organize them and bargain for them unless we represent *everyone* in the plant, no matter how miserable, craven, and clueless the others may be.

Why?

"Well, it's the law, isn't it?"

No, no, no: there's no law that says in order to bargain the union has to be the exclusive representative of everyone, including a Tea Party type who might be spying for the boss. As AFL-CIO general counsel Craig Becker said, even *before* the Wagner Act there was never a law that barred an employer from signing a contract that applied *just to members of the union,* distinct from *everyone in the plant.*

Even before the Wagner Act came along in 1935, there was members-only bargaining.

So what did the Wagner Act add?

Passed in 1935, the Wagner Act said, first and above all, that people had a right under federal law to engage in collective bargaining without being fired and without reprisal. As plain as daylight, Section 7 of the Wagner Act says that employees covered by the act have a right "to engage . . . in concerted activies for mutual aid and protection." That means they have a right to do these things *without being fired or disciplined.* In Section 7 the word "union" does not appear at all. Indeed, employees do not even have to be trying to form a union.

In law school, the very first Section 7 case I read had nothing to do with a union. A guy walked in and complained to the boss, "We're cold out there. Turn up the heat." Annoyed by the whining, the boss fired him. That's all legal, right? No. "But he wasn't trying to bargain, he just said, 'I am cold.'" To the contrary, he did not say, "I am cold"—he said, "*We* are cold." That word "we" brought the case under Section 7. And by saying "we," he was thereby engaged in "concerted activities for mutual aid and protection."

"You mean if you complain about the heat, you can't be fired?"

Yes, if we have the wits to say "*we*," then we can't be fired.

The same is true if we go out on strike, even if no "majority" union or any union is in the offing. Take the baristas at a Starbucks. If two or three baristas walk out in the morning rush, even at 8:50 a.m. with a line out the door, the two or three have a legal right to strike without being fired.

"Does it matter if the baristas even *want* to organize a formal union?"

No.

"If the two or three *claimed* to be a union, would it be against the law to bargain with them over *their own* wages, so Starbucks could get them back?"

No.

"And this is all legal?"

Yes, when two or three are gathered together, they have a lot of rights under the Wagner Act—they can even walk out and come back without being fired. I know most people think, "Come on, of course Starbucks can fire people who walk out with ten customers in line. In fact, can't it just fire people for being *late*?" Yes, it can fire any *single* barista for being late—unless he or she is part of a group acting collectively. For some I know this will be the single hardest part of this book to understand. So let me repeat it: Starbucks cannot fire those two or three baristas if they are acting collectively.

Should I say it again? They can't be fired.

The confusion arises because the baristas can be "replaced," permanently, *during the time that they are out on strike* and ten customers are in line—that is, if Starbucks has time to advertise for and interview applicants. But if the baristas go out for an hour around 8:30 a.m., or for a day, or two days, and then return to work, and if Starbucks has not yet hired anyone, then the baristas have the right to go right back to work—and without any discipline. Starbucks can't even put a bad mark on their records.

In fact, even if Starbucks manages to hire a new barista in time but that barista eventually quits, the striking barista gets back the job. After all, legally, that striking barista was never "fired."

Another source of confusion is one I mentioned in an earlier chapter: that union members who *are* under contract paradoxically do not have the same legal right to strike. That makes no sense, right? The people whom one would most expect to have the right to strike have no such right at all—at least while a contract with a no-strike clause is in effect. And if the no-strike clause is not explicit, the courts imply it anyway. So if the barista at Starbucks were under a union contract, and that contract had a no-strike clause, Starbucks could fire him.

But he's not in a union: and the more labor shrinks, the more we have the right to strike, for five minutes, ten minutes, any time of the day.

So let's go back to Chattanooga. If the Starbucks outlet down the street from me can't fire three baristas who go out on strike, you can bet Volkswagen can't (and won't) fire several hundred high-skilled people who go out for a short strike. In fact, I doubt it would even refuse to bargain in the first place, as long as the UAW were willing to settle for being a "nonmajority union" and negotiate for just those willing to be dues-paying members. After all, that's what Volkswagen does in Germany with IG Metall. Over there in Europe, it's all members-only bargaining. So why wouldn't Volkswagen do it over here? Indeed, Volkswagen has signed a contractually binding "declaration" that it will engage in such bargaining on a worldwide basis. The relevant part of Section 1 of "The Declaration on Social Rights and Industrial Relations at Volkswagen" states: "The basic right of all employees to establish and join unions . . . is acknowledged." If that's so, one might ask, why doesn't Volkswagen bargain with the UAW now? Well, unlike IG Metall and most European unions, the UAW wants to be recognized as the union representing *everyone*. It wants more than the members-only bargaining to which Volkswagen could plausibly claim this declaration applies. Volkswagen could say that the whole system in the United States is different: after all, by recognizing the UAW as the exclusive representative for everyone, it is conferring on the UAW quite a prize, something no German or other European union could get. So long as the UAW insists on being the exclusive representative, at least on the money issues, then Volkswagen has an out—or can *say* it has an out. It can ask that the UAW either prove beyond doubt that it represents a majority or require a secret-ballot election.

As long as we cling to Section 9(a), every employer has an excuse to do nothing—until there is a secret ballot-election following a "campaign period" in which some union busters will do everything but burn crosses on people's lawns.

"But if a union is *not* the exclusive representative, does the employer have any legal duty to bargain with less than a majority of its employees?"

And here is the big objection: if the UAW is not the exclusive representative, does the Wagner Act require the employer to bargain at all?

Well, if we are talking about employees who are not UAW members, then no, Volkswagen has no legal *duty* to bargain with the UAW about *those* employees. And the UAW may have no right to engage in such bargaining for *those* employees.

What about those who *are* UAW members?

There is at least a reasonable argument that Volkswagen does have a legal duty to bargain with a nonmajority union. Let me explain the legal issue as best I can: under Section 8(a)(5) of the Wagner Act, an employer has a duty to bargain collectively and in good faith, but over the years many authorities have come to believe that the legal duty under Section 8(a)(5) kicks in only when the labor union has become the "exclusive representative" after the formal NLRB election and the whole shebang.

The problem is: nothing in the text of Section 8(a)(5), not a word, limits the duty to bargain only to unions that are certified under Section 9. Logically, such a limitation would make no sense. For example, if the baristas have a legal *right* under Section 7 to engage in bargaining, it seems to follow that Starbucks should have a legal *duty* to bargain in return—at least with those baristas who want to exercise their legal right. Again, nothing in the Wagner Act says otherwise.

Still, for years most have believed that the duty to bargain arises only when there is a union officially certified under Section 9 as the exclusive representative. The unions themselves seem to take that view; and, like many labor lawyers, I used to think so too. Lately, though, thanks to Professor Charles Morris of the Southern Methodist University Dedman School of Law, a lot of us are doing a rethink. In 2011, a who's who of labor law professors led by Professor Morris filed a petition for the NLRB to declare that Section 8(a)(5) required an employer to engage in members-only bargaining, or bargaining with a nonmajority union that was not the exclusive representative. Nothing came of the petition; it was withdrawn, in part because the NLRB was not even functioning at the time, with Senate filibusters blocking nominees to the board.

However, now the Morris petition is likely to be refiled. And now that the Senate has ended filibusters of presidential nominees, Obama could appoint board members who could require such members-only bargaining. After all, Professor Morris—a onetime editor in chief of *The Developing Labor Law*, a kind of bible for labor lawyers—has a good case. He has set out his argument in a book, *The Blue Eagle at Work: Proclaiming Democratic*

*Rights in the American Workplace* (2005). His recitation of the early New Deal history is especially telling. Even after 1935, the CIO unions that did the mass organizing did not purport to be the exclusive representatives. I suppose I always knew that—there were no card checks or secret-ballot elections in 1937. What I did not realize was that employers like U.S. Steel and GM negotiated those first agreements to apply to actual dues-paying members and no one else.

"Wait—how could they cut a deal for just union members without applying it to everyone else?"

That's right—how could they? So they didn't. They just voluntarily applied it to everyone, even though some workers were not covered in the contract. Just as employers do in Europe, they extended these members-only contracts to everyone, even if the union members had the only real contractual rights. That's still the case now with Volkswagen and BMW and Daimler when they negotiate in Germany.

So why does everyone else get the same deal?

Think about it: it's in the employer's interest. Let's put aside wages. If GM or U.S. Steel or Volkswagen said that the grievance procedure applied *only* to dues-paying union members, there would be a rush to join the union. That's not what employers want. It's the last thing the National Right to Work Legal Defense Foundation wants. Why would GM or U.S. Steel or Volkswagen in Wolfsburg want to do something that would build up the union treasury, even apart from the problem of administering such a contract for some and not others?

The extension of the contract is paradoxically a way to limit unionization. That's why there is so much contract extension in Europe, while there is virtually none here. Yes, it's true that in some countries, such as Belgium, the state encourages the extension of these contracts. But that's not true in all of them, and Germany is one of the big exceptions.

To sum up: In Europe, "entry" into a bargaining relationship is easy. Get two or three baristas to sign up at a single Starbucks outlet, and at least technically, in terms of starting a bargaining relationship, you're good to go. In the United States, entry into this same relationship is nigh impossible. We have to sign up and get the votes of a majority of baristas—and not just at one outlet but at maybe seventy across Chicago, if the NLRB decides that is the appropriate unit for Section 9 certification, or maybe seventy thousand across the nation, if *that* is the appropriate unit.

And please note: with this approach, there is no incentive for a "contract extension" to other Starbucks locations. No, Starbucks can claim the extension of the "bargaining unit" would not be "appropriate" under the law, and then both parties are off to years of litigation. And of course, inside these "appropriate bargaining units," whatever they turn out to be, either everyone gets the contract or no one gets it—and this is only in that unit. Outside of that ministate in which the union is declared the exclusive representative, the only way to extend to the next Starbucks is to go through a whole new campaign again. To be sure, it may not get that ridiculous, but it often *does* get that ridiculous.

The right couldn't dream up a better system.

"Yes, it's all the right's fault, isn't it?"

No, it's the fault of the left, or at least it's partly our fault. It's our organized labor, the AFL-CIO—our home—that insists on a Section 9 process. Historically, as Professor Morris says, one can trace the turning point back to the 1940s. That's when unions became addicted to a Section 9(a) certification.

Why did labor get addicted? Follow the money, at least the dues money. Once there was a Section 9(a) certification, the money rolled in. There was no risk. You didn't have to keep persuading people to stay in the union. Naturally, no union wanted to organize any other way.

It is the fault of the right for blowing up the system, but it is the

fault of the left for not backing off and trying another way. Professor Morris is too circumspect to say so, but we have probably screwed ourselves.

"Yet does a union have any power when it represents just 30 percent?"

My European friends might say, "A union of 30 percent may have *more* power." If the union tries to represent everyone, it's more timid, it's lumbering, it steps on its message. How can it be otherwise if it is representing people who don't want to be in a union at all? Compare it to how politicians will sound in a primary election and how they sound in a general. If the union is 30 percent, if it is nothing but the true believers, it is more militant; it has a sharper message. And it may be more inclined to strike. To be sure, with 40 percent, it is *much* harder to shut down a plant indefinitely, but no one is likely to conduct that kind of strike anymore. The twenty-first-century strike is much more likely to be short term and strategic, an attempt to disrupt and then scramble back. And for this kind of strike, a union might be more effective representing just 40 percent who will approve of this tactic than trying to win over everyone in the plant. Or to take the case of Volkswagen: the most pro-union employees, so I am told, are the "maintenance" guys. No, these are not janitors but high-skilled troubleshooters who "maintain" the production line. If they leave for a few hours, everything shuts down. Why not start members-only bargaining with the highest-skilled employees around? Shed of the burden of a Section 9 certification, a union can be nimbler and more militant than before.

That's the real answer to those who would deny that Section 8(a)(5) applies to members-only bargaining. Who cares? If the 30 percent have the power to disrupt, and if they have a legal right to strike *without being fired*, then the employer has good reason to bargain. And if the 40 percent do not have the power to disrupt, it probably won't matter whether there is a "duty" under Section

8(a)(5) or not. After all, Section 8(a)(5) doesn't require the employer to agree to anything.

As a labor lawyer, I know the appeal of a Section 9 certification. It's easier to budget. It's easier to assign staff. I get it. Well, we'll just have to be poorer. And more union-side lawyers like me have to go without work. It's also like a Maginot Line: With that Section 9 certification, no one can dislodge "my union," or at least not without bringing up really big guns to mount a "decertification" campaign. Without Section 9 to provide cover, it's cold and lonely out in those plants—and who back in the union office knows for sure what is going on?

So giving up Section 9 is no easy thing. Believe me, I would never argue for giving it up where it already exists. Nor would I argue for giving it up when we can plausibly get it. Professor Morris suggests that members-only bargaining can be just a phase—a kind of way station—on the way to a Section 9 certification. He is not saying—and please, *I* am not saying—that members-only is the only way.

But the day may come when it is the only way. By the time this book comes out, the scare may be over, but the case of *Mulhall v. UNITE HERE* has given everyone a shock. I have failed to mention that there is an antibribery statute, Section 302 of the Labor Management Relations Act of 1947. As drafted broadly, Section 302 is a criminal law that prohibits the employer from giving a "thing of value" to an employee representative, i.e., a union officer. In *Mulhall* a Florida casino offered a "neutrality agreement" to a union in return for the union's support on a gambling referendum. The National Right to Work Legal Defense Foundation claims that a neutrality agreement—an agreement to use card check—was a thing of value, and the casino had committed a crime under Section 302. Why? The use of card check to get a Section 9 certification was a thing of value to the union.

The Supreme Court took the case and then dismissed the

appeal for technical reasons. That is, the Court let the decision stand, and so this interpretation of Section 302 of the LMRA is the "federal law" only in the states that make up the Fifth Circuit. It is still not federal law in the other ten circuits, at least for now. Some think this is a victory for labor, because the Court did not affirm the Fifth Circuit but just dodged the issue. I think it is more like a disaster, since the Supreme Court probably would have reversed—narrowly, by 5 to 4—because this interpretation of Section 302 is not just absurd but unworkable. That's just my guess—I say that because three liberal justices dissented from the dismissal and no doubt sensed that if the Court got to the merits, it would reverse as a matter of common sense. (Apparently, Justice Kennedy, who is the swing vote, was hostile to the use of Section 302 in this way.)

But I could be wrong, and a wild argument from the far right has a way of going mainstream over time. It is possible to imagine a day when a slightly tweaked version of the current Supreme Court upholds this far-right view of Section 302. From that point on, logically, *anything* of value to a union becomes illegal, even if it is a wage increase for its members. Forget about card check. A wage increase itself could be a thing of value. Any collective bargaining agreement could be a thing of value. Under this view of Section 302, taken to the extreme, any concession by an employer to a unionized workforce could possibly be a crime.

As I said, I don't think *Mulhall* will survive. I also do not believe that Section 302 will ever be read so as to criminalize literally every intangible thing of value to an employee representative—even going so far as to encompass a good contract to the union official who negotiated it. Surely even the far right will stop at such an absurdity. Won't it?

Still, things look pretty bad. Now that the Supreme Court has let *Mulhall* stand, I can understand why employers like Volkswagen, even if located outside of the states in the Fifth Circuit, will hesitate to recognize any union as the exclusive representative until the issue is resolved. After all, *Mulhall* may one day be the law of the land. So the choice right now is: a secret-ballot election or members-only bargaining. And yes, it could go beyond *Mulhall*. Here in this book I just wish to record that, in these dark days for labor, one could see how far one could take Section 302 if even more conservatives get on the Supreme Court.

I would offer every fatted calf and make every burnt offering to keep any such thing from happening. Decisions like *Mulhall* are just too absurd. But I admit to a little part of me thinking: Fine. Go ahead. Let them do it. Let them declare it all illegal. While I don't believe I'm saying this, I hereby go ahead and do so: Let the right put us back where we probably should have been a long time ago, alongside the teachers, marching through the streets.

# 12

# Why We Live in Hope

Day to day, I go from annoyance with just about everyone in organized labor to a religious-type awe at the way it now brings in the
best people I'll ever know. Maybe as labor gets weaker, with less
clout to offer, it's attracting more mendicants and holy ones, readers of Hermann Hesse novels, seekers after the truth. I suppose
it's a sign of labor's collapse that so many of the people in it seem
nicer. Really, I could write a whole book knocking labor for its
hacks and timeservers, but it would be hard to find better people
than Leo Gerard at the United Steelworkers or Bob King at the
UAW. It pains me to say that even the AFL-CIO is better; indeed,
it now has some astonishing idealists. To be sure, there are still
the louts, some out-and-out gangsters, and labor itself has a long
way to go before it represents John Dewey's idea of extending a
democratic way of life. The very enfeeblement of labor may be
the biggest threat to democracy within it—that is, the weakness
if not irrelevance of labor makes it all seem beside the point. Let
me give just one example. In the 2011 Teamster presidential election, an unpopular president, James Hoffa, faced two strong chal-
lengers. It should have been the election of the century. But only

maybe 10 percent of the rank and file bothered to vote. "They don't think it makes any difference," a Teamster local president said. And it will seem to matter less and less until people see that a labor movement able to change their lives really has come back. That's how Dewey might put it: there is no labor movement for the same reason there is no real democratic "public." When one comes back, so will the other.

I write this book for people who will never buy it. It's for people who know little or nothing about—or care little or nothing for— labor unions, but who may care about ensuring the United States is a going concern. Let me review again the reasons that even these people have for bringing back a labor movement, on the politically conservative grounds that it is the one way to hold the country together. Labor is the only way to deal with the fault lines in our country's economy. I set out those reasons in chapter 6.

*First*, absent going into debt, we don't have paychecks big enough to sustain the kind of aggregate demand that will keep us near full employment. We would have to dig too deep into our pockets to get spending up enough to bring unemployment down to 4 percent. The rich take the income and then sit on their money. Indeed, as we dig into our pockets, they want to lend it to us—at credit card interest rates. I hope it is clear that by aggregate demand I mean not just consumption but investment as well. Without a labor movement to pump up people's paychecks, business will not spend. We need a labor movement to help recycle the financial surplus that is piling up in our companies.

*Second*, without a labor movement we'll continue in debt as a country—because we don't produce enough. In terms of our trade debt, we're the biggest debtor country in the world—a terrible problem about which both political parties are more or less in denial. We're in debt in this way because of a shareholder model from which working people and even most of the managers are excluded and that is accountable to no one—not even to the stockholders any longer, certainly not to the country, which has a strong national interest in a corporate model that will keep us out of external debt. Rather, our current corporate model erases accountability to anyone but accountants, who are charged with ensuring the biggest short-term profit. The financial people who now run our companies cut and cut till some of the corporations that should be our global champions are unable to compete. We need to move from a shareholder model to a stakeholder model that is accountable to people who might have pride in what they're doing—or at least have some commitment to keeping the company in existence. We need a corporate model with a form of worker control or voice—enough to check the bonus culture that lets Bain Capital types line their pockets and does not press them to invest. Then we can start to right our still wild imbalance of trade, notwithstanding the fact that we may soon be massively exporting oil. With the right institutions, we can have an economy that is not export-dependent but can compete on equal footing with countries that are, such as Germany, Japan, China, Taiwan, and Korea, among others. We need what the stakeholder economies have: namely, a real "partnership" between labor and management, albeit one in which labor is very much the weaker partner but at least present in the boardroom with some limited say.

*Third*, we need a labor movement that will both directly and indirectly shrink the financial sector. The point is not to end inequality but to transform the country into something other than a creditor/debtor society. Only a labor movement can hold back the growing crowd of us lining up to borrow. That's crucial to our survival—the more we line up to borrow, the less competitive the country becomes. As Keynes argued, the rich would rather part with their money by lending it out to us at interest than—as he put it so elegantly—using it to employ us in the construction of durable goods. This is another way of saying that we need a labor movement not only to get the middle class out of debt but also to get the elite to invest.

*Fourth*, we need a labor movement to ensure the fiscal stability of the state. Our private debt is potentially our public debt, just as our public debt is potentially our private debt. We will just keep moving it from one set of books to the next. Look at Ireland and Spain: those countries had massive private debt in 2008, while the governments had practically none. When the crack-ups came, that private debt turned into public debt. It doesn't matter on which set of books we put the debt. If the private sector is on the verge of bankruptcy, as in 2008, even a government that *looks* solvent—one that has no debt—is effectively on the verge of bankruptcy too. I can say to Tea Party types and deficit hawks, all of you: only a labor movement can get the government out of debt.

*Fifth*, we need a labor movement to jolt the political debate out of magical thinking. It's not just the Tea Party that lives in a fantasy world; the Democrats do too. It's laudable to promote higher education, but it's delusional to think that formal education by itself, absent any institutional change, is going to address the serious structural problems in our economy. Is a college education important? Sure. But a college education is a weak predictor of whether the diploma holder can manage his or her own finances— look at how we're running up student debt. It is a weak predictor of whether the diploma holder will pick up a newspaper or go to the polls to vote. It has no validated effect—no effect, none—on the debt level of the country, the trade deficit, or any of our other serious problems. Yes, it's a political "fact" that "independents" like to hear about education as an answer to our economic woes, but "independents" have only a fitful engagement in our politics, and they expect to "hear" about education as the answer because that's the only answer our political class ever gives them.

Perhaps here I should apologize again for using Germany as a model. Many—not all, but many—Americans just plain dislike Germans. Whether that is a fair judgment, historical animus, or bigotry I will let other people decide. But whatever our feeling about Germans, it should not stop us from engaging in rational thinking. I am not proposing that we like or admire them personally and go hang out in Berlin, only that we learn from them. And the one thing we can learn is the central position of a labor movement in directing a free-market economy that is not being run by the state. Germans can be grumpy about their unions—as people normally will and should grump about any human institution—but at least they, or the elite, or some cross section of the country, understand the importance of a labor movement. I emphasize: it's a cross section. Some Americans say: "But isn't it because they have a labor party in Germany?" It is more accurate to say that in Germany they have *four* labor parties: the CDU, the SPD, the Green Party, and the Links could all claim with some justice to be labor parties. In the United States, it is arguable that not even the Democrats are a labor party. Some may like to think this stakeholder model is something for Nordic types or Germans, just a product of national character. But in reality, it is nothing but a form of modernization, which in the twenty-first century we reject at our peril.

Finally, let's get to the most urgent reason to bring back a labor movement. We need it to deal with the fault lines in our Constitution and keep not just the economy but the Republic itself from cracking up. No reader of the *Federalist Papers* will miss the point: without some mechanism for the have-not faction to possess real power, our constitutional balance is out of whack. In *Federalist* No. 10, James Madison argues that the design of the Constitution is to achieve a balance between the majority have-not faction and that of the haves.

But what happens if the have-not faction isn't even suiting up for the game?

That's why I'm for *any* kind of labor movement, even old labor, with all its flaws, hunkered down in D.C. I'm glad it's there. In the short run, we need old labor, if only to save Social Security and Medicare. But for these two programs, what else is holding our federal union together? In the short run, we need the old labor, just to have a fair fight over the future of the country.

In the long run, we need something fundamentally new. We need the kind of labor movement that will extend Dewey's vision of a democratic way of life: at school, in the workplace, in the ways we treat one another. May I say one more thing about the famous Dewey-Lippmann debate? It is sometimes said that no one won. But I think there was a winner. Lippmann after all argued that it was not possible for the country really to change: people in the 1920s were disengaged and frivolous; they paid no attention to anything serious. Dewey argued then and at other times that it would be otherwise if people were not so powerless. This was a debate over whether democracy is really possible, based in part on what Dewey and Lippmann saw people reading in the papers.

Lippmann, a journalist, scoffed at the press of his day, the era of bathtub gin, with all its celebrity tattle, swooning over Valentino. How could what people read in the papers prepare them to make serious decisions? Dewey could mumble about democracy as a method of social inquiry, but the only inquiry some could see was into the lives of movie stars.

It seemed for a while that Lippmann had the better of the argument. But there was not much of a labor movement in the 1920s, and by the 1940s it was a different country. People were engaged. And that's a revelation I had one day when I was down in my mother's basement.

Down in the basement was a blown-up front page of a local paper on the day my parents married. Of course I'd seen this page on the wall before; it was the *Cincinnati Times-Star* from

April 12, 1947. But this time, I looked closer and started to read the stories.

As I read, I was startled. This front page I was reading seemed to vindicate Dewey. Even on a Saturday afternoon, in 1947, this front page showed the kind of democracy in which he so much believed.

What first hit me was all the text: far more than today. I counted nine *hard* news stories, genuinely "fluff free," which is a better batting average than the front page of the current *New York Times*.

But here was the much bigger surprise: the subject matter. I'd say half the stories were directly or indirectly about labor. To be sure, the big lead of the afternoon, "KENTON COUNTY IMPOSES BAN ON BINGO," was "nonlabor" enough (unless they had the bingo in the union halls). But the second lead was a labor story: "PHONES MONITORED UNION TELLS U.S./FCC Asked to Investigate/Pickets Here Put on a 24 Hour Basis." And there were more labor stories: "SENATE GOP TO OFFER LABOR BILL" was one. Even "BODY RAPS NCH BOARD MAJOR" turns out to have been a labor story. So was "FRUIT VEGETABLE DRIVERS WALKOUT APPEARS UNLIKELY." And in the national news, the big story was arguably about a labor or working-class hero, Henry Wallace: "WALLACE SPEECHES shocking/Vandenberg Sharply Criticizes Ex Vice President."

These were serious stories: densely written and even, well, fair and balanced. It would be unthinkable today that most college-educated people would pick up anything with as much text, much less a paper with so many stories about labor.

It's depressing to pick up a *RedEye*, the *Chicago Tribune* spin-off that younger college grads in my Southport neighborhood tend to read: a daily paper with lots of cleavage, covering the latest doings of vampires in Hollywood.

Consider this: on April 12, 1947, just about the time of the passage of the GI Bill, nearly all of the readers of the *Times-Star* would have stopped their education after high school. Many would be high school dropouts.

How could people in 1947 with so little education have gotten through all this text?

But consider this as well: the writers for these papers were high school graduates too. My friend Steve Franklin, who started as a reporter in 1970, was shocked to find that even at that time most of the senior reporters had never been to college. It's strange to think that a reporter like I.F. Stone, who so dazzled grad students in the Vietnam era, never went to college. Did higher education levels lead to a more substantial press than Lippmann could imagine? No. It's not that our education improved. The New Deal did not care about education in a formal sense. But by 1947, it had raised the education level of the country by engaging people in decisions.

Dewey *was* right. Here's what I think he might tell us now. "All our cheerleading for higher test scores, or even for more kindergarten and pre-K, will be in vain, useless, and do nothing to raise the real education level, our engagement in our democracy, until we let people into the making of decisions." I hope Dewey wouldn't consider such a statement too direct. Nor has the Internet made us much more of a democracy. Yes, it's nice that some of us can go off into a cubicle and blog, and never engage each other face-to-face, but even if technology has accidentally let more people into the debate, it doesn't do much good until we also let them participate in the making of more decisions.

But it really is a good thing we can broaden the debate. It may sound hopeless, but here's what we can do: focus on changing the way that the leaders of the Democratic Party talk. That's not so impossible. The Constitution, written or unwritten, does not prohibit it. Force them to say, finally, at last, it's not just all about education: we must change the corporate structure of our firms as well. *Say it.* Force them to say that there is too much hierarchy, and we have to lift the weight of that hierarchy that keeps pushing people down. Follow through on the Bain Capital commercials, at least in how we talk about the problems of the country.

That was the goal of the civil rights movement: not just to change the law but to change the way the leaders of the Democratic Party talked—indeed, even the way some Republicans of the day talked. Despite all the money in our politics, it is possible to change the cowardly way we now avoid the real challenges of our day.

Maybe it will take a strike, or a series of strikes, or some other kind of disruption; maybe it will happen just because we are embarrassed by our level of inequality. It's not just income inequality, though that is part of it. Europeans who visit and go into our workplaces are shocked by the hierarchy, and they are right to be shocked.

We have to change not just the country but the way we live. We have to figure out, in our own time, with a new kind of labor movement, how we can lead a democratic way of life. Unless we do so, you and I are done.

But we're not done, not yet. We're going to come back as something new.

—Thomas Geoghegan
July 30, 2014

# Index

# About the Author

**Thomas Geoghegan** is a practicing attorney and the author of several books, including *In America's Court: How a Civil Lawyer Who Likes to Settle Stumbled into a Criminal Trial*, the National Book Critics Circle Award finalist *Which Side Are You On? Trying to Be for Labor When It's Flat on Its Back*, *See You in Court: How the Right Made America a Lawsuit Nation*, and *Were You Born on the Wrong Continent? How the European Model Can Help You Get a Life*, all published by The New Press. He has written for *The Nation*, the *New York Times*, and *Harper's*. He lives in Chicago.

# Publishing in the Public Interest

Thank you for reading this book published by The New Press. The New Press is a nonprofit, public interest publisher. New Press books and authors play a crucial role in sparking conversations about the key political and social issues of our day.

We hope you enjoyed this book and that you will stay in touch with The New Press. Here are a few ways to stay up to date with our books, events, and the issues we cover:

- Sign up at www.thenewpress.com/subscribe to receive updates on New Press authors and issues and to be notified about local events
- Like us on Facebook: www.facebook.com/newpressbooks
- Follow us on Twitter: www.twitter.com/thenewpress

Please consider buying New Press books for yourself; for friends and family; or to donate to schools, libraries, community centers, prison libraries, and other organizations involved with the issues our authors write about.

The New Press is a 501(c)(3) nonprofit organization. You can also support our work with a tax-deductible gift by visiting www.thenewpress.com/donate.